REFORM THOUGHT IN SIXTEENTH-CENTURY ITALY

AMERICAN ACADEMY OF RELIGION

TEXTS AND TRANSLATIONS SERIES

James A. Massey, Editor

Number 4

REFORM THOUGHT IN SIXTEENTH-CENTURY ITALY

Elisabeth G. Gleason

ELISABETH G. GLEASON

REFORM THOUGHT IN
SIXTEENTH-CENTURY ITALY

SCHOLARS PRESS

Distributed by
Scholars Press
101 Salem Street
P.O. Box 2268
Chico, California 95927

REFORM THOUGHT IN SIXTEENTH-CENTURY ITALY

Edited and Translated by
Elisabeth G. Gleason

© 1981

The American Academy of Religion

Library of Congress Cataloging in Publication Data
Main entry under title:

Reform thought in sixteenth-century Italy.

(Texts and translations series / The American
Academy of Religion ; no. 4)
Bibliography : p.
Contents : Statutes of the Oratory of Divine
Love of Genoa, 1497 — Three letter of Gasparo
Contarini to Paolo Giustiniani and Vincenzo Querini,
1511-1523 — Dialogue concerning the thief on the
cross, 1542 / Bernardino Ochino — (etc.)
1. Reformation — Italy — Addresses, essays,
lectures. 2. Counter-Reformation — Italy — Addresses,
essays, lectures. 3. Theology — 16th century —
Addresses, essays, lectures. I. Gleason,
Elisabeth G. II. Series: Texts and translations
series (American Academy of Religion) ; no. 4.
BR390.R43   230'.0945   81-5648
ISBN 0-89130-498-3 (pbk.)   AACR2

Printed in the United States of America
1 2 3 4 5 6
Edwards Brothers, Inc.
Ann Arbor, Michigan 48104

TABLE OF CONTENTS

PREFACE

The present volume is intended as an introduction for American students to a relatively little known area of sixteenth century European religious thought: Italian writings about reform of the individual and institutions. These themes were discussed or written about in all countries at the time, and Italy was no exception. Yet Italian contributions to the great debates of the Reformation period are known mostly to specialists.

There are two reasons for this. First, given the usual curricular patterns in American universities, the entire Reformation era is rarely accorded more than one semester or quarter course. Thus little time remains for exploring anything besides the central aspects of religious and intellectual history. Second, there is a great dearth of Italian sources translated into English. Even instructors who would like to call the attention of their students to Italian thinkers have difficulty finding available materials.

I have tried to remedy this situation somewhat by presenting here a few examples of a rich and complex tradition of thought. My hope is that some students will be drawn to Italian religious history of the sixteenth century and will begin exploring it on their own. The bibliography that concludes the volume should be useful for this purpose.

I have translated all pieces except the *Beneficio di Cristo*, an excellent modern English version of which is included with the permission of the President of the Unitarian Historical Association, The Casa Editrice Felice Le Monnier in Florence, and the gracious consent of the translator, Dr. Ruth Prelowski Liebowitz. I am grateful to them, as to friends and colleagues who helped me with difficult passages. The errors remain mine, of course. Each piece is prefaced by a brief introduction, and the reader's attention is called to the most important secondary

sources.   The annotations should elucidate the meaning of
most allusions or unclarities in the texts.   Finally, I
realize that my translations all too frequently lack grace;
my only excuse is that many of the pieces were not written
in an elegant style in the original Italian or Latin, and
that I have tried to be as accurate as possible while presenting at least readable English versions.

INTRODUCTION

The pieces selected for inclusion in this volume
illustrate the variety of ideas about reform of the individual and institutions in sixteenth-century Italy. The
authors range from an uncompromising proponent of the
Counter-Reformation like Gianpietro Carafa at one extreme
to the radical exile Camillo Renato at the other. Their
views concerning almost every aspect of Christian doctrine
differed widely. What united them was an ardent desire
to bring about change in the ways people practiced their
Christian faith and in the church which taught and guided
them toward salvation. To Carafa, the visible church under
firm papal leadership had to be purified of abuses. Only
then would it truly fulfill its mediating role and deal
effectively with the menance of heresy. Renato, too,
espoused the ideas of a pure church. But for him it was the
community of those who have faith, for whom outward struc-
tures, even the sacraments, are unnecessary, since God's
grace works directly on the elect.

The arrangement of the selections deliberately does not
separate their authors according to their adherence to
Catholicism or Protestantism. Some committed reform thinkers
remained members of the Roman church, while others left it,
seeking a more evangelical form of Christianity in northern
countries. Whatever their ultimate fate, all were deeply
concerned with the relation of men to God, and formed part
of the movement for religious reform in Italy, which included
much more than the Counter-Reformation or the responses to
ideas of northern reformers.

The translated sources that follow are divided into
three groups. The first has as its focus a personal concern
for reforming the individual so that he can draw nearer to
God and better understand what constitutes the Christian life.
How that life is defined ranges from placing oneself in the

service of God and neighbor within the framework of a lay
confraternity to a submergence of the self in contemplation
of the suffering Christ on the cross. A common assumption
runs through these pieces, different though they are in
their purpose: that reform, turning away from sin and
indifference, must begin with the individual Christian and
then penetrate the social and ecclesiastical hierarchies.
Their authors thought that a change of heart bringing about
true repentance was a deeply personal matter; it did not
result from institutional guidance, but from the working of
grace in the soul.

In contrast, the second section presents two proposals
for changing existing institutions. Both assume that Rome,
the center of Christianity, must be purged of abuses before
a new spirit can pervade the body of Christendom. Reform
must begin with the head, the pope and curia, and continue
with the members of the Christian church. The memorial of
Gianpietro Carafa is among the clearest expressions of this
way of thought. The piece that follows it bears the marks
of a committee report. Its authors were not as absolute in
their judgment as Carafa.

The tracts in the third part directly challenge the
conceptual framework of the existing church of the time.
The first, the *Beneficio di Cristo*, certainly the most
famous literary product of Italian reform thought, is a
complex document that reflects not only the urgency with
which ideas of justification were discussed, but also the
influence of northern reformers and of the Spanish religious
writer Juan de Valdés. The concluding treatise by Camillo
Renato which follows is an example of radical reform thought
which disregarded traditional doctrines and institutions as
meaningless to true Christian life.

No Italian ruler supported the Reformation, nor did a
single state become Protestant. In 1542 the Roman Inquisition, reorganized and centralized, began dealing effectively
with religious dissent. The decrees of the Council of
Trent, which closed in 1563, further strengthened the

Counter-Reformation. Growing religious uniformity replaced
the diversity of reform thought, some aspects of which this
collection illustrates.

I. The Question of Personal Reform
and the Christian Life

1. Statutes of the Oratory of Divine Love of Genoa (1497)

A. Introduction

The first Oratory of Divine Love was a confraternity
founded in Genoa in 1497 by Ettore Vernazza, a layman deeply
influenced by St. Catherine Fieschi-Adorno, and his three
friends, Giovan Battista Salvaigo, Nicolo Grimaldi, and
Benedetto Lomellino. It was composed of a majority of lay
members and a few priests who took upon themselves the
obligations of regular prayer, participation in the liturgical and sacramental life of the church, and performance of
charitable works. Similar oratories were established
shortly afterward on this pattern in Rome, Brescia, and the
Venetian territory. They emphasized the care of the sick,
especially the so-called incurable suffering from syphilis,
the establishment of hospitals, charity to the poor, to
orphans, to former prostitutes, and aid to criminals condemned to death.

Older scholarly works presented the Oratories as cells
of Catholic reform before the Protestant Reformation.
Especially the Roman Oratory, founded in 1516, was long
considered an important center of reform thought, supposedly
with members such as Gasparo Contarini, Jacopo Sadoleto, and
Gianmatteo Giberti, all of whom became cardinals and
conspicuous advocates of church reform. This picture had to
be modified after the papers of Bartolommeo Stella, one of
the first to join the Roman confraternity, were found and
published in 1948. They included a list of the Roman members
in 1524. For the most part, the latter were obscure men;
none of the prelates mentioned above belonged to the Oratory.
Gianpietro Carafa and St. Gaetano da Thiene, the co-founders
of the Theatine order, were members, as was the poet
Marcantonio Flaminio. But the importance of the various
branches of the Oratory clearly does not lie in the number
of leading reformers it included.

Much more significant is the nature of the Oratories'
spirituality. Their primary purpose was moral reform and
regeneration of the individual members, and the "planting
of divine love" in their hearts, as the statutes so simply
express it. From the love of God would flow the love of
neighbor and concern for his spiritual and physical welfare.
Thus the ideal of the Oratory was the fostering of living,
personal faith, and a translation of Christ's teaching
concerning one's fellow-man into a program of action. This
strong awareness of the social dimensions of Christianity
forms a link between the Oratories of Divine Love and the
many new orders with a practical orientation founded in the
early sixteenth century.

However, the statutes show that the Oratory had deep
roots in the past. Its spirituality was traditional, and
so were its forms of devotion. The medieval practice of
scourging as a means of penance persisted in the Genoese
Oratory, and possibly in the Roman one as well. Its ideal
of individual reform included old and new elements, pointing
to the question concerning the nature of lay spirituality
and the role of lay confraternities in the wider context of
sixteenth-century Italian religious history.

The most significant modern contribution to the history
of lay confraternities, their background and spirituality,
is Giuseppe Alberigo, "Contributi alla storia delle confraternite dei disciplinati e della spiritualità laicale nei
secc. XV e XVI," *Il Movimento dei Disciplinati nel Settimo
Centenario dal suo inizio (Perugia, 1260)* (Perugia: Deputa-
zione di storia patria per l'Umbria, 1962), pp. 156-252.
The following are also useful: Gabriel Le Bras, *Études de
sociologie religieuse*, Vol. II (Paris: Presses Universitaires
Françaises, 1956), pp. 418-462, two essays on the history
and structure of religious confraternities; Gilles Gérard
Meersseman, "La riforma delle confraternite laicali in
Italia prima del Concilio di Trento," *Problemi di vita
religiosa in Italia nel Cinquecento. Italia sacra. Studi
e documenti di storia ecclesiastica*, Vol. 2 (Padua:

Editrice Antenore, 1960), pp. 17-30. Pio Paschini, "Le
Compagnie del Divino Amore e la beneficenza pubblica nei
primi decenni del Cinquecento," *Tre ricerche sulla storia
della Chiesa nel Cinquecento* (Rome: Edizioni Liturgiche,
1945), pp. 3-88. Alfredo Bianconi, *L'opera delle compagnie
del "Divino Amore" nella riforma cattolica* (Città di Castello: S. Lapi, 1914). P. Francesco Saverio da Brusciano,
O.F.M. Cap., "Maria Lorenza Longo e l'opera del Divino
Amore a Napoli," *Collectanea Franciscana*, XXIII (1953), pp.
166-228. For a brief, informative discussion of lay
confraternities retaining the practice of scourging in
Northern Italy, especially Venice, see Brian Pullan, *Rich
and Poor in Renaissance Venice* (Oxford: Basil Blackwell,
1971), pp. 34-40. Helpful: Giancarlo Angelozzi, *Le confraternite laicali* (Brescia: Editice Queriniana, 1978), pp. 7-
71.

   The statutes were translated from Pietro Tacchi-Venturi,
Storia della Compagnia di Gesù in Italia, 3d ed. (Rome:
Civiltà Cattolica, 1950), Vol. I, pt. 2, pp. 25-35.

B. Text

   Art. I.

   In the name of our Lord Jesus Christ the statutes of
the Confraternity of Divine Love, under the protection of
Saint Jerome, begin here.

   Brethren, our confraternity is instituted for no other
purpose than that of rooting and planting divine love, that
is charity, in our hearts. Therefore it is called the
Confraternity of Divine Love, also because charity proceeds
only from the gentle look of God, who regards none but the
humble of heart, according to the word of the prophet:
"Whom shall I regard but the humble, who fears my words."[1]
Therefore, whoever wants to be a true brother in this
confraternity must be humble of heart. All practices and
principles of our confraternity lead to humility. Therefore
let everyone direct all his mind and hope to God and love
him completely; otherwise he would be lying and false

brother and make no contribution to this confraternity which
can bear no fruit that does not pertain to the love of God
and neighbor. This should suffice as to the name. Above
all let it be understood that whatever is contained in these
statutes, or others which might be added later, is not
binding on penalty of sin, especially mortal sin.

Art. II. Concerning the Father Prior.

As there is one God in heaven, and one Shepherd [*i.e.*
the pope] on earth, so it is fitting that among you there
should be one head whom all the members shall obey. Among
you he shall be called Father Prior, and you will owe him
respect as to a father, and true obedience. He shall hold
office for six months only, at the end of which he shall
have the same standing as the other brethren, and be unable
to become prior or hold another office for a year and a
half. Great caution should be exercised in his election;
you should pray that the Holy Spirit may enlighten you to
choose him who above all others has placed his trust in
God and possesses those other qualities that belong to a
devout prudence. There should be among you no one who dares
to solicit the vote of any brother for himself or for others.

[Then follow instructions about the procedure to be used
in elections of the prior and his two counselors.]

Art. III. Concerning the election of three assistants
and other officials.

[Procedures for electing assistants to the counselors,
visitors to the infirm, dispensers of alms, the master of
novices, and other officials.]

Art. IV. Concerning the powers of the prior and the
three assistants.

[The prior may impose various kinds of penance and tax
the members; neither he nor his assistants may sell real
estate belonging to the confraternity, receive novices on
their own, establish a new branch of the Oratory, or alter
the articles.]

Art. V. Concerning the number of brothers and religious.

Since there is confusion where there is a multitude, the
number of brothers may not exceed thirty-six laymen and four

priests. . . . This number cannot be changed unless four-
fifths of the brothers, present in the oratory, vote in
favor of it.

Art VI. Concerning the office of visitors of the sick.

Since we would be of little avail to the brothers unless we perform the spiritual as well as corporal duties of
brothers toward each other, "since the proof of love lies
in its manifestation by works,"[2] therefore whenever one of
our brothers is sick one or more visitors should gladly go
to visit and help him, especially spiritually. If he is
indigent, they should provide him with the necessities at
the expense of the confraternity. If asked, they should
stay the whole night taking care of him, providing him with
a doctor and medicines; above all they should arrange for
his confession and communion, as they would do for themselves. If it is necessary to spend money, they may spend
without permission what seems appropriate to them. They
should ask the brothers, either singly or together, for
help for this sick and poor brother. If they cannot provide
otherwise for such a necessity, then they can with the
consent of the prior sell and alienate some of the movable
property of the confraternity. But they should especially
and with all diligence seek to aid him spiritually in such
extreme straits. In addition to this office, the said
visitors, or others in their place, should distribute
available alms among the poor, especially those of our
confraternity. If necessary, they should ask the other
brothers for help.

Art. VII. Concerning the office of caretakers.

[To open and lock the oratory and keep it clean and
neat.]

Art. VIII: Concerning the office of the syndic.

[He is the treasurer and keeper of records.]

Art. IX: Concerning prayer, offices, and ceremonies.

Since prayer and devotion are what unites us with God
and enables us to obtain all graces, all brothers who are
eager to fulfill their duties should be urged to turn their

heart and mind to God when they rise in the morning, offering themselves to him with great love, and asking that he
direct their steps all through the day according to his
will. Every day, remembering the seven canonical hours[3]
when Jesus Christ our Lord suffered his bitter death for us,
the Lord's prayer should be said aloud seven times in a
heartfelt way, and similarly the *Angelus*. Everyone shall
always say the Our Father and Hail Mary before meals.
Getting up from the table, he shall say: "But you, o Lord,
have mercy on us."[4] In addition, every Monday all shall
recite five times the Our Father and the Hail Mary for the
souls of the departed brethren. These are the ordinary
prayers which everyone shall say at least daily. Then on
Saturdays or Fridays, or other days chosen by the prior and
counselors, as well as on the vigil of Candlemas, the vigil
of Pentecost, the vigil of the Assumption, the vigil of our
glorious protector St. Jerome, and the vigil of All Saints,
you shall assemble in the oratory, and in accordance with
instructions set forth in the next article, recite the usual
office. On Holy Thursday the brethren shall assemble after
the meal; while they are assembling, some devotional work
shall be read. Then the foot-washing shall be performed with
the ceremonies found in the book of offices, or with others,
as the prior sees fit; then the great matins[5] shall be recited and the scourging done in the usual way. When one of our
brethren passes from this life, the office of the dead, or
at least the first nocturn[6] for his soul should be said in
the oratory on a day determined by the prior. The priests
should each say a mass for his soul, and the other brethren
for twelve continuous days should recite for him the *Miserere*,
De profundis, *Deus in nomine*[7] with three Our Fathers and
three Hail Marys, or else fifteen Our Fathers and fifteen
Hail Marys daily, or at least they should pay a *soldo* to
the treasury for his soul. Besides this, everyone should
remember [in his prayers] the departed brethren as frequently
as possible. Every year on the eve of All Saints Day the
brethren should assemble in the oratory and say there the

office of the dead, or at least the first nocturn for their
souls. The priests among us should each say a mass for them
within eight days. The same should be done on a day during
Lent, as the prior determines. After the office the names
of the dead brethren shall be read, and everyone should
answer: "May they rest in peace."

    Act X: Concerning good practices.

    Men who publicly or secretly lead bad lives cannot be-
long to your confraternity: those who keep concubines,
usurers, the unjust, and blasphemers. Let no one of you
gamble, or be present at games of dice or cards or other
prohibited games, or even those permitted on account of
cupidity. When the divine office is chanted in church, let
no one of you stroll around, striking up conversations:
you should not talk with each other more than is proper in
holy and respectable places, but must always set a good example to each other and to those who see you. In the oratory
everyone should call his brother "Sir," even though he might
be younger. If you hear that one of the brethren has fallen
into sin, first try to make him turn away from it. If you
don't succeed, tell the prior, who should use means that
seem suitable in order to bring him back. For the sake of
sound discipline everyone should fast one day a week, if
possible. Other than [stressing the fast on] the vigil of
St. Jerome, our protector, or else that of St. Michael, I
will say nothing about vigils and other days of obligation,
for I presume that everyone will fast on them. Holy days of
obligation should be spent doing spiritual works, since they
were ordained for that purpose. On other days everyone
should hear mass, if possible, or at least be present at the
elevation of the host.

    When a brother enters the oratory on a meeting day, he
shall say softly "Peace be with you" as he sits down. When
four fifths are present, one should read from a devotional
work. When it seems appropriate to the prior (or to him
who is taking his place), a signal should be given; the

reader should stop and genuflect before the prior. Everyone
shall keep silence; then the service should begin.

     If a brother comes after the service has begun, he shall
kneel down in the middle of the choir and not move unless
the prior gives a sign. Whoever comes after the first psalm
should be prepared to receive punishment. After the service
the lights will be extinguished. The brother who has read
the lesson before will go to the altar and begin the prescribed reading, and then say: "Make use of the scourge."
The [other] brothers will scourge themselves, while he
recites the *Miserere*;[8] when it is finished, together with
the usual [biblical] verses and prayers, the prior will make
a sign when he sees fit, and the scourging will stop. The
brother lector will read a section from the Passion until
the prior gives a signal. Then the cantors will recite:
"Now dost thou let thy servant go in peace," and when they
reach the passage: "This is the light which shall give
revelation,"[9] one of the caretakers will bring a lighted
candle. Then the hymn of the coming Sunday or feast-day
should be recited, together with verses and prayers for
these feasts.

     After the service is finished, and while the prior is
still at the altar, the syndic will read the names, if any,
of those brothers who were not present at the first psalm.
They shall come forward to the altar. [Then he will proceed
to the names of those] who failed to come one or more times
to the oratory, played at cards or dice in contravention of
the statutes, were present and watched while the said prohibited games were played, did not recite the Our Father
and Hail Mary while sitting down at table and "But you, o
Lord," while rising from it, did not say five Our Fathers
and five Hail Marys on Mondays for the souls of the departed
brethren, did not say seven Our Fathers and seven Hail Marys
daily at the seven canonical hours, did not daily look at the
body of the Lord [in the Eucharist], strolled through the
church during the chanting of the divine office, did not go
to confession during the past month, broke the silence, did

not fast one day a week, or did not perform the penance
imposed by the Father Prior at the appropriate time and
place.

Art. XI: Of Confession and Communion.

Each brother should go to confession as frequently as
he can, at least once a month. This he is obliged to do.
He should take communion at least four times a year, in
addition to Easter and Christmas. The first time he should
do it on Candlemas, the second on Pentecost, the third on
the feast of the Assumption of Mary, the fourth on All Saints
Day. This should be done in our oratory, if possible. Let
everyone come with devotion and purity of heart, as is proper
for such a great sacrament. On the vigils of these feasts
the brethren should assemble and recite the usual office as
set forth above.

Art. XII. Concerning novices.

When it happens that someone wants to invite another to
join our confraternity, he should let the prior and the
counselors know. The prior will give the name of the candidate to the master of novices, who shall make diligent
inquiries about him for one month. Having obtained the
available information, he will communicate it to the prior
and the counselors, who among them will take a vote whether
to pass it on to the brethren. If there is a two-thirds vote
in favor of doing it, the prior will do so. The brethren
will seek to inform themselves about the candidate during
two months. Meanwhile the prior will frequently pass on
this information to [all] brothers. After two months have
elapsed, the matter shall be put to the vote. If those who
vote for him are in the majority, the master of novices or
whoever seems appropriate to the prior and the counselors
shall seek to speak with the candidate and show him our
statutes, telling him how glad he was to hear that such a
confraternity exists elsewhere, and that its statutes have
come into his hands. If the candidate is well disposed, [he
should be told] that maybe such a confraternity could be
established here; thus, if he is not interested, he will not

know that it has already happened. After this a vote shall
be taken, if the prior and the counselors wish it; if four-
fifths of the ballots are in favor of the candidate, he
shall be invited to the oratory. First the master of novices
should examine him, and if he finds him firm of purpose, he
shall bring him along on an evening which suits the prior.
On that evening there shall be no services, but only the
reception of the novice, according to the appropriate procedures. The novice shall offer a candle weighing about
two pounds and take the last place in the choir. No one
under twenty-two years may be admitted, unless it should
appear to the prior, the counselors, and the three assistants
that an exception should be made because of a person's good
behavior, habits, and reputation. In that case he must be
at least eighteen years old. In the admission of novices
great caution should be used so as not to choose unworthy
persons.

Art. XIII. Concerning the general meeting.

As in every ship there is a drain through which the
impurities are flushed out, so in every confraternity ways
and procedures are necessary by which to purge bad offshoots.
Therefore every year during Lent the prior shall announce
a day on which he intends to call a general meeting and order
the brethren to come after they have gone to confession. On
that day all the brethren shall be voted upon, one by one,
and each brother shall cast his vote in the case of every
other one. In order to remain, a person must receive three-
fourths positive votes [of all that are cast]. While a vote
is being taken, the person under consideration must leave
the room. Everyone shall be obliged to keep secret whatever
is said about the absent brother, on pain of exclusion from
our confraternity. [Then follow voting regulations to be
employed in the case of someone who has revealed secrets to
outsiders.]

Art. XIV. Concerning secrecy and punishment of those
who reveal the names of brethren, and other matters.

Since this is a confraternity of laymen who sometimes

shy away from good works because of what others say, therefore every member shall be obliged to keep secret the names
of his brethren and the works and ways of the confraternity.[10] If someone hears that a brother has revealed anything about the confraternity, he must tell it to the prior.
The latter shall be obliged to look into the matter together
with the counselors if he deems the accusation to be true,
as well as to decide whether they should judge him by taking a vote. If then three-fourths of the votes go against
him, it shall be understood that he is excluded from the
confraternity; if they do not, he shall do such penance as
the prior, the counselors, and the three assistants impose.
In this case the three assistants may exceed the authority
they ordinarily have in matters involving penance, and may
condemn him to pay a fine of up to ten pounds. Someone
who was disobedient or did not want to perform the acts of
penance imposed on him shall be dealt with in a similar
manner. However, he shall first be admonished three times
by the prior or by other brothers chosen for this task by
the prior, to the glory of God and the whole heavenly host.

2. Three Letters of Gasparo Contarini to
Paolo Giustiniani and Pietro Querini (1511-1523)

A. Introduction

Gasparo Contarini (1483-1542) was born of an ancient
Venetian noble family. Embarking on a career of public
service in 1518, he was Venetian ambassador to Emperor
Charles V from 1521 to 1525, and to Pope Clement VII from
1528 to 1530. He made a particularly favorable impression
at the papal court by his learning and probity. Upon his
return to Venice he filled various important offices, including that of head of the Council of Ten, until in May,
1535, Pope Paul III made him a cardinal. Contarini there-
upon took holy orders and during the next years worked in
Rome on several commissions drawing up proposals for reform
of the church and the curia. In 1541 he was sent to the
Diet of Regensburg as papal legate, where a colloquy of
Catholic and Protestant theologians made an unsuccessful
effort to bring about doctrinal concord on such crucial
issues as justification. From January, 1542, until his
death on August 24, he was papal legate in Bologna.

Already as a young man Contarini was interested in the
two fields which were to remain his favorite subjects of
study all his life: philosophy and theology. During his
years at the University of Padua from 1501 to 1509 he devoted
himself above all to the systematic reading of Aristotle and
his commentators, and eventually wrote several philosophical
works. He also studied theology, turning especially to the
issues of reform of the church and of the individual Christian. After the outbreak of the Lutheran Reformation he
became a spokesman for concord with the Protestants and advocated the necessity of purifying the Catholic church of
abuses for the sake of peace and harmony among all Christians. His conciliatory attitude at the colloquy of Regensburg made him suspect to the intransigent opponents of

21

Protestantism at the papal court despite his affirmations
of loyalty to the Roman church.

Contarini deeply felt the contradiction between theory
and practice in the church of his day. His desire for reform of its head and members found repeated expression in
his works beginning with the writing of his treatise *On the
Office of the Bishop* in 1517. But the origin of this concern, which lay in the nature of his own religious develop-
ment, remained unknown until thirty of his letters dating
from 1511 to 1523 were found in the library of the Camaldolese monastery near Frascati and published in 1953.
Written without any stylistic elegance to two of his closest
friends, both Venetian nobles who had joined the strict
Camaldolese order, they reveal the length and intensity of
the spiritual struggle waged by Contarini in his search for
assurance of God's mercy and forgiveness. He discusses in
a deeply personal way the old questions of whether a man
engaged in secular affairs can become inwardly reformed
and lead a true Christian life, and what the nature of such
a life should be.

The letters enable us to understand the basis for his
later attitudes, and are significant as an Italian example
of the same kind of widespread spiritual anxiety that tormented the young Luther at almost the same time. Contarini,
too, arrived at the conviction that man is justified not
by works, but by faith in the merits of Christ's suffering
and death. However, this realization did not prevent him
from remaining a firm supporter of the papacy as an institution. He decided to work for reform from within the
Catholic church and submitted himself to its teaching and
discipline.

The most useful bibliographical introduction to
Contarini is James Bruce Ross, "The Emergence of Gasparo
Contarini: a Bibliographical Essay," *Church History*, 41
(1972), pp. 22-45. See also the same author's "Gasparo

Contarini and his Friends," *Studies in the Renaissance*,
XVII (1970), pp. 192-232; Felix Gilbert, "Religion and
Politics in the Thought of Gasparo Contarini," *Action and
Conviction in Early Modern Europe. Essays in Memory of
E.H. Harbison*, ed. by Theodore K. Rabb and Jerrold E.
Seigel (Princeton: Princeton University Press, 1969), pp.
90-116; Gigliola Fragnito, "Cultura umanistica e riforma
religiosa: Il 'De officio viri boni ac probi episcopi' di
Gasparo Contarini," *Studi veneziani*, XI (1969), pp. 75-189.
The standard biography remains Franz Dittrich, *Gasparo
Contarini* (Braunsberg: Druck und Verlag der Ermländischen
Zeitungs=und Verlagsdruckerei, 1885).

The letters are translated from Hubert Jedin, *Contarini
und Camaldoli* (Rome: Edizioni di Storia e Letteratura, 1953).
This publication, designed as an "Estratto" from the
Archivio Italiano per la Storia della Pieta, vol. II
(1953) consists of 67 folio pages, numbered pp. 3-67. The
second volume of the *Archivio* did not appear until 1959,
and contains the letters on pp. 53-117.

B. Text

1. Gasparo Contarini to Paolo Giustiniani.
Venice, 24 April [1511]

Reverend and beloved Father.[1] Already some days ago
I received your letter, full of that loving kindness toward
me which I have always known you to feel.

During the past holy days at San Giorgio,[2] where I
stayed with Messer Vincenzo Querini,[3] I read several of
your letters. To tell you the truth, with one side of my
mind I was extremely pleased with them, since I realized
your ardent desire to serve God. I know indeed that this
service surpasses even the greatest earthly lordship because his Majesty does not require it for his benefit. God
is in himself infinitely more perfect than our mind can
comprehend (not that I could write about it so briefly),
and he cannot receive any benefit from our service. But
because our ultimate happiness lies in serving him and in
submitting ourselves to his will in everything, he asks
this service of us.

Seeing your progress along the way of humility, where
you seek to humble yourself as much as possible, I was
greatly pleased. I truly believe that for someone who
dedicates himself to good works nothing can be as harmful
as self-satisfaction. For this ill no better remedy can
be found than humility.

All these and many other things have given me great
consolation, as has your good will toward me which I see
increasing rather than diminishing, and which I know I
do not deserve.

Although outwardly I seem to you to have qualities for
which I deserve to be loved, alas, if you knew me inwardly
as I really am, and as even I don't know myself, you would
not judge me [as favorably] as you do.

Outwardly I have lived in such a way, far from [doing] good works, as to deceive not only you but also myself. I persist in my self-deceit, persuading myself that I am good, living in the midst of continuous wicked deeds, and persevering in them. But now no more of this.

What you have written has pleased me very much. Yet, on the other hand, I read what you so sincerely wrote: that after having left the whole world for the love of Christ, and after living such an austere life, you still fear that your sins committed in the past are such that you cannot do suitable penance for them during the remainder of your life. I saw you dwelling on these thoughts and fears. Because of this I turned to myself to examine my own life during the past years, only to see that I have a disposition which will not adapt itself at all--and I don't mean to the kind of life you lead, but even to the barest approximation of it. It does not allow me to escape the multitude of the city [Venice] and find a little solitude which is plentiful in any religious order, or to leave my friends and relatives who live here. I am telling you truthfully that I was quite discontented and very nearly desperate when I considered all this.

Still, hope lived in me, saying: "What do you know? Maybe you could have a change of heart; greater miracles than this have happened." However, when I saw how hardened my heart was, I was troubled.

On Holy Saturday I went to confession to San Sebastiano,[4] and spoke for a long time with a saintly monk. Among various topics of discussion, almost as if he had known my troubles, he began to tell me that the way of salvation was broader than many people think. Not knowing me otherwise, he talked with me at length.

Leaving from there, I myself began to think about eternal happiness and about our condition. I really understood that, if I did all possible penance and much more besides, it would be of no avail to render satisfaction for past sins, let along merit eternal happiness.

God, who is never-ending goodness and eternally burning
love, has seen this. He loves us worms so much that our
mind cannot grasp it; having made us out of nothing only
through his goodness, he has lifted us to such heights
that we can share that happiness in which he is always
happy in himself. Besides original sin, God has seen our
many other sins; if no satisfaction were made for them with
penance and sorrow it would not be fitting for him who is
perfect justice to admit us to the heavenly Jerusalem. As
if impelled by most fervent love, he wanted to send his
only-begotten Son to render satisfaction through his passion
for all those who desire him for their guide and want to be
members of the body of which Christ is the head. Although
all cannot have so much grace as to be members close to
the head, still all those who are connected with this body
by an influx of the powerful satisfaction which our head
has rendered can hope to give satisfaction for their sins
with little effort. Only we must strive to unite ourselves
with Christ our head in faith, hope, and the little love of
which we are capable. His passion has been enough and more
than sufficient for the satisfaction for sins committed and
those into which our human frailty continues to fall.

By this thought my great fear and sadness were transformed into cheerfulness, and I began turning with my whole
mind to God, who is perfect goodness. I saw him hanging
on the cross with outstretched arms for love of me, and with
his side open even to the heart, so that if I, miserable
creature, should not have so much determination as to be
able to leave the world and do penance for the satisfaction
of my iniquities, I still might turn to him. Provided I
asked him to make me a sharer in the satisfaction which he,
without sin of his own, has rendered for us, he is immediately ready to accept me and to move his Father to remit
completely the debt I have incurred, and which I could never
satisfy through my own efforts.

Shall I not then sleep securely, although in the midst
of the city, and although I may not have repaid the debt
which I contracted, since I have such a payer of my debt?
Truly I will sleep and live as securely as if I had spent
all the days of my life in a hermitage, with the intention
of never abandoning this consolation.

And yet, if sometime I were to abandon him (which I
hope will never happen), I have the firm intention of returning immediately, seeing him always holding his side
open even to the heart for me, and of loving him ever more,
if I can. My heart shall at all times praise him and extoll
his goodness. And if I shall not always be able to love
him with tenderness, at least I will always wish to love
him more than I can. I will seek with my whole heart to
put all my hope and affection in that ever-burning love.
And so I shall live securely, without any fear of my wicked
deeds, because his mercy surpasses. all his other works.

I have written you all this in order to rouse my feelings and soften my hardened and obdurate heart, and because
such have been my thoughts; I have told you the unadorned
truth. Although I don't disapprove of your fear because it
is indeed the cause of keeping you humble, still (and this
is the tyro teaching the master) I shall persist in remind-
ing you not to let your thoughts dwell on it too much.
Rather, after thinking about it for a while, turn more
frequently to the other thoughts [about which I wrote] and
ponder them day and night. Thus neither the memory of your
iniquities nor the day of judgment will perturb you so as to
extinguish completely the living hope which you will have.

It has seemed well to remind you of all this, albeit
presumptuously, because I have experienced it myself, finding that hope is of much greater profit to me than fear.
The latter led me to sadness and almost to despair. Such
perturbation could considerably trouble you who live in
solitude. So let all your thoughts dwell on [God who is]
perfect love, hoping and believing firmly that if we

approach him even a little with our love, no other great
satisfaction is necessary, since he has given satisfaction
out of the depth of his love for us.[5] And in this thought
I, to whom not even a tiny bit of determination is given to
do what you are doing, but who live in the crowd of the
city, sustain myself and always shall do so. I hope and
always shall hope in this satisfaction; otherwise I would
be in a dark mood.

    Let us therefore live joyfully, because freed from this
fear we can serve God all our days. I shall remind you,
although it is superfluous, to remember me in your prayers.
Affairs are still not settled so that we have not decided
on the time to come and visit you. I pray the Lord to give
us peace, if it is for the best.[6]

    Farewell in Christ, Reverend Father, and remember me.

                  Your Gasparo Contarini

      2. Gasparo Contarini to Paolo Giustiniani
    and Pietro Querini. Venice, 17 July [1512]

Most venerable Fathers![7] Since I would like to discuss
the same thing with both of you, it did not seem right to
separate you through my letter, whom the same place, way
of thinking, and affection always keep closely united. I
do not want to be wordy and bore you. You both know how
three years ago, after I left the University of Padua for
Venice on account of the war[8] and became tied to you by
a closer friendship than before, I had the firm intention
of finishing the study of human philosophy to which I had
already devoted much work. Then I planned to turn to
Christian learning, and studying it to spend my years
quietly in the fear of the Lord.

    Having finished with the former subject, I next turned,
I don't know why, to the study of mathematics and the
theology of St. Thomas. I worked assiduously for two
unbroken years especially on mathematics, but also on
theology. I continued to review some philosophy with my

friends whom you know. Thus I have been looking forward
most eagerly to finishing the study of human sciences
which I had resolved upon. I was hoping to lead then a
joyful and tranquil life, engaged in the kind of study that
cheered me when I only thought of turning to it.

Now that the study I had undertaken is finished and the
longed-for time has come, I have fallen into that melancholy
disposition from which I have already suffered greatly, as
you know. I believe this happened because of impatience
with my studies during the past year. Although less
intensely than before, I am still bothered with such sad
and disturbing thoughts and such terrifying fancies (I
mean terrifying because of things that reason maintains to
be almost impossible), that I believe few people are found
in the world with a more restless mind than mine.

I have come to hate my studies, and the only thing which
at other times cheered me up, the reading of Sacred Scripture, now troubles me greatly. Moreover, it seems to me
that I will be constrained to change my way of life, and I
believe the time will never come when I can quietly
meditate on the Scriptures, which at other times used to
kindle my heart. It is almost as if it had palled on me
and is the reason my melancholy has come over me.

I find myself in this state, and already for over two
months I have been living in idleness, seeking feasts and
amusements as much as possible, because the physicians
advise me thus. However, on the one hand I am troubled by
my body, and on the other by dark thoughts, the more so
since the only remedy I had proposed to myself against
all misfortune, namely Sacred Scripture, now gives me no
consolation. I am afraid that the time may never come
when I shall love it.

You see clearly, my Fathers, brothers, and friends, the
miserable state of your friend and brother through your
kindness. Although I do not at present nor ever will
despair of divine mercy and goodness and the merits of
Jesus Christ crucified, nevertheless I place great hope

in the prayers of friends and servants of God, which you
are. I know that you have particular affection for me
besides your charity toward all Christians in our blessed
Lord Jesus Christ.

With what effectiveness I have recourse to you, you can
decide yourselves. I beseech you that in your prayers you
condescend to implore Jesus Christ crucified, our true
mediator, to deign to free me from my affliction and perturbation of mind, from vain fears and the temptation which
has come over me, so that because of this disease I can no
longer hold fast to his teaching and live a life dedicated
to his service.

Although I tell myself that it is not possible (even
though now, because of my sins, he permits me to doubt it)
that, while contemplating that which is perfect sweetness,
in which no bitterness is found, bitter feelings should
arise in me, and that, while putting all my hope in him who
alone is strong, terrifying thoughts could come into my
mind, still at times I give in to those whispers that say
in my heart: "There is no salvation for him in his God."[9]
Then I answer continually: "You, o Lord, are my defense, my
glory, and the lifter up of my head."[10]

At other times I think: "Since it pleases the Lord that
I should not be able to entertain happy thoughts of him,
as do the most perfect, who taste no other sweetness than
the perfect good, I will live in amusement and pleasure,
observing as much as lies in my power his law in matters
that are mortal sins. Thus I will enjoy the world because
this sadness is too bitter for me." And in this thought I
find rest.

Still I hope that maybe, when I shall least expect and
believe it, his goodness will deign to rekindle my heart, to
drive out every vain fear and restlessness, and make
my soul clear, pure, constant, and strong, so that I will
be able to say to myself: "My heart is fixed, trusting in
the Lord; my heart is established; I shall not be afraid,
until I see my desire upon my enemies."[11] I do not know

when that will happen; only he knows.

I believe that his Majesty, apart from my excess in study and the continuous occupation of my mind without any respite, has allowed me to fall into this affliction for no other reason than to teach me that becoming calm and tranquil does not depend on me as I believed. Madman that I was, who thought that after having finished the study of human sciences I could will to live content and tranquil! But the name of his Majesty be praised for everything.

I would be grateful if not only the two of you, but also the Father Hermit[12] and other monks, whom you might ask, would pray for my intentions. Console me by your letters, as I expect, and do not propose any [new] difficulty of austerity in my way of life for now, since by so doing you would lead me almost to despair. Only continue to stress the love of Jesus Christ for us, urging me to trust that even in the multitude of my sorrows within me his comforts shall delight my soul.[13] And cite appropriate examples which could deeply move me.

I would like to know how Father Thomas is, who suffered similar, although still more intense difficulties; did he experience such perturbations of mind, and how did he overcome them? Such examples, which had a happy outcome, comfort me wonderfully. But one should express oneself briefly to the prudent and to friends! Farewell, happy souls, and remember me in Jesus Christ.

Your Gasparo Contarini

3. Gasparo Contarini to Paolo Giustiniani.
Valladolid, 7 February [1523]

[Thanks him for his kind letters, and excuses himself for not having written sooner. Has waited with longing for Giustiniani's letters; their admonitions are always fruitful. His brother-in-law Matteo Dandolo wrote that he lost some letters of Giustiniani, which he was supposed to forward to

Contarini, and enclosed others. Contarini is sending
various letters to Giustiniani, among them one from the
Emperor to Pope Adrian VI (Jedin surmises that it was
in support of Giustiniani's new monastic foundations)].

Now I will tell you something about myself, my great
physical troubles, and the even greater ones of the mind.
At the end of May we departed from Flanders,[14] travelling
by way of England, where we remained until July 6. I
passed the time with our Suriano,[15] and suffered many inconveniences as well as running the danger of disease, both
in London and in Southampton.

Beginning with the above-mentioned day of July, and in
keeping with the usual good luck of the Emperor, we had
perfectly calm weather and crossed the sea in ten days.
We landed in [the Bay of] Biscay, in a port called
Santander, from where we proceeded to cross the Pyrenees,
which are truly rugged mountains, and arrived on the
Spanish plain. We have been staying here in Valladolid
for five months already, suffering the greatest inconveniences as far as our lodging and provisions are concerned.

Such has been my trip, accompanied by great bodily
hardship. I shall not add anything concerning the distress
of the mind, but will let you imagine it, since you know
my affairs.

But I shall always praise even more than I am able to
express it the goodness of God, which has guided events in
a better way than anyone would have imagined, so that peace
has been preserved until now. I trust that it will not
abandon me and my work in the future.

Now enough about the troubles of public affairs.

Different disorders continually afflict my mind, which
is vacillating and indeed most unsettled. I simply cannot
write about them in detail; but someone who is wise and
experienced in the affairs of the world, as you are, is able
to know what they are. I have truly arrived at the following firm conclusion; although I had formerly read it and
knew how to repeat it, nevertheless only now, as a result

of experience, do I fully grasp its meaning. It is this: nobody can justify himself or purge his soul of worldly affections through works. We must have recourse to divine grace which we obtain through faith in Jesus Christ, as Saint Paul writes, and we must say with him: "Blessed is the man to whom the Lord will not impute sins, without works."[16]

Consequently, I understand the ancient philosophers clearly: although they saw the truth in the idea that purification of the soul from desires is necessary for happiness, and said so, nevertheless they were capital fools in thinking that this purification could be brought about through habit, by acquiring the habitual practice of virtues that suppress worldly affections. Now I seem to see through my own example as well as that of others that man falls down more easily precisely at the point when he thinks he has acquired these virtues. From this I conclude that any man that lives is but nothingness[17] and that we must justify ourselves through the justice of another, namely Christ. Joining ourselves to him, his justice becomes ours. We must not trust ourselves at all but say: "For ourselves we could find no outcome but death."[18]

I would very much like to know your thoughts about this matter because, to tell you the truth, after my experience with myself and the realization of what my capabilities are, I have taken refuge in this thought alone; all the rest seems as nothing to me.

Maybe I have been more long-winded than you would have liked. Pardon me. The pen has gone on without my noticing it. Pray to God for me that he may guide me in public as well as private affairs. Farewell and remember me.

                              Your Gasparo Contarini

3. Bernardino Ochino, *Dialogue Concerning
the Thief on the Cross* (1542)

A. Introduction

Bernardino Ochino was born around 1487 in Siena.
Little is known about his family and early life. As a
young man he decided to enter the Observant branch of the
Franciscan order, which eventually disappointed him because
of its laxity. His desire for a rigorous religious life
led him to join the newly formed Capuchin order in 1534.
Its founder, Matteo da Bascio (1495-1552), wanted to follow
closely the example of St. Francis by a return to his simplicity and austerity. Ochino was attracted by the ascetic
life of the Capuchins, and as one of them greatly added to
their reputation by the excellence of his preaching as
well as the example of his life, which many contemporaries
considered a model of saintliness.

In 1538 Ochino was chosen general of his order. His
fame was great throughout Italy, and he was so much in
demand as a preacher that in 1542 the Pope himself had to
decide in which city he would preach during Lent and Advent.
Fra Bernardino usually confined himself to gospel texts and
stressed the central position of Christ. Critics of his
approach were not lacking, as for example in Modena in 1540,
when he was accused of preaching too much about Christ and
of failing to mention even once the patron saint, San
Geminiano. But this kind of criticism was voiced by a few
dissidents in a wave of great enthusiasm for his preaching,
which contrasted favorably with the generally low level of
ordinary sermons.

On his repeated visits to Naples, Ochino came to know
the Spaniard Juan de Valdés, whose religious thought influenced him deeply. Valdés was the center of a circle of
laymen seeking a deeper and more personal Christian spirituality than conventional practices offered. To this group

35

belonged noblewomen such as Vittoria Colonna, Isabella
Bresegna, and above all Giulia Gonzaga, who was closest to
Valdés. The nature of Valdés's thought and his influence on
the religious life of both Italy and Spain in the sixteenth
century are still debated. What deeply impressed Ochino was
the Spaniard's insistence on faith in the benefits of
Christ's death and on interior reform of the individual, together with his indifference to dogma or exterior practices,
and ultimately to the whole structure of the church.

It is not certain at what point Ochino began reading
Protestant works. Between 1536 and 1542 he was several
times accused of spreading heretical ideas, and Cardinal
Alessandro Farnese, the grandson of Pope Paul III, eventually summoned him to Rome. Ochino feared that he would
have to justify himself against the suspicion of heresy,
and in August 1542 he fled to Geneva. He married and had
a family. Until his death in 1563 in Austerlitz (Moravia),
in the house of Niccolo Paruta, another Italian religious
exile, Ochino led a difficult life. Unable to agree with
Calvin, he left Geneva for Germany and from there continued
the wanderings of a man whose religious ideas became
increasingly radical and suspect wherever he settled.

Everything Ochino wrote belongs to the period of his
exile with only two exceptions: *Nine Sermons*, printed in
Venice in 1541, and *Seven Dialogues*, which appeared there
in 1542, and which includes the dialogue translated here.
It is a precious document of Ochino's views before his
formal break with the Catholic church. He stresses faith,
trust, love of Christ, and especially the memory of his
passion; the individual Christian will not be saved unless
he, too, like the thief, undergoes a true inner conversion.
Many of his readers accepted these ideas, believing that
they were compatible with the teachings of the Roman church.
It was still a period before clear lines were drawn separating Catholic and Protestant teaching.

On Ochino, see Karl Benrath, *Bernardino Ochino of Siena.*
A Contribution Towards the History of the Reformation
(London: J. Nisbet & Co., 1876); Ronald H. Bainton,
Bernardino Ochino, esule e riformatore senese del Cinque-
cento, 1487-1563 (Florence: Sansoni, 1940); Benedetto
Nicolini, *Bernardino Ochino e la Riforma in Italia* (Naples:
R. Ricciardi, 1935); and *Il pensiero di Bernardino Ochino*
(Naples: R. Ricciardi, 1939); Gigliola Fragnito, "Gli
Spirituali e la fuga di Bernardino Ochino," *Rivista*
Storica Italiana, 84 (1972), pp. 777-813, an outstanding
contribution to the understanding of Italian reform groups
around 1542; Philip McNair and John Tedeschi, "New Light
on Ochino," *Bibliothèque d'Humanisme et Renaissance,* 35
(1973), pp. 289-301.

The following dialogue is translated from: *Dialoghi*
Sette del Rev. Padre Frate Bernardino Ochino Senese, Gener-
ale dei Frati Cappuccini. Biblioteca della Riforma
Italiana, Vol. V (Florence: Claudiana, 1884), pp. 53-60.

B. Text

Speakers: A Man and A Woman

Woman: Who is not astounded to see the depth of divine
judgment? Christ was hanging on the cross all lacerated,
close to death, turned down by Pilate, betrayed by Judas,
abandoned by others, persecuted by the Jews, scorned by
gentiles; everyone lost faith in him except his afflicted
mother, the glorious Virgin Mary. And now a poor thief
began to believe in him, when the others lacked faith, those
who had spoken with Christ, heard his evangelical doctrine,
seen his innocent life, his supreme virtues, his over-
abundant charity, his complete, holy, and profound humility,
his prodigies, signs, and miracles, read the prophets,
studied the Scriptures, seen the prophecies [of the Old
Testament] and everything fulfilled in Christ, and with
all that did not believe in him. Not only did he hang on

the cross without performing miracles, but he did not show
himself as glorious through divine deeds when a poor, blind
and ignorant thief[1] who had not read or seen the Scriptures,
without signs and miracles, neither having seen nor heard
Christ before, himself on the cross with such great pain
and suffering, seeing Christ suffer so much and being close
to death, believes that he is God and hopes to receive
paradise from him who said on the cross: "My God, my God,
why have you forsaken me?"[2] I would like you to tell me
from where this great faith of his came.

   Man: Some said that Christ's shadow fell toward him,
and he was illuminated by it; as Saint Peter healed the
sick with his shadow,[3] so Christ illuminated him because
not only has Christ, the light of the world, illuminated us
sufficiently with his teaching and his life, but his shadow,
namely the Old Testament, which is the shadow of the new,
is sufficient to give us the necessary light of the divinity
of Christ. Some said that the Virgin was on the side where
the thief was; she looked at Christ and he at her, and the
radiance of their glances passed near the thief, illuminat-
ing him.

   Woman: Tell me, what do you think about it?

   Man: The good thief, looking at Christ, saw him suffer
so much without being troubled; on the contrary, with a
happy face he seemed to rejoice in shedding his blood. He
saw burning tears falling to the ground and ardent and
fervent sighs rising to heaven. He heard his loving words,
contemplated his divine deeds and actions, his admirable
patience, his great charity, long perseverance, and other
divine virtues, by which he was led to believe that he was
truly the Son of God. God cannot fail him who turns to
him. The thief disposed himself according to his weakness,
but Christ illuminated him. If the other thief had also
been disposed as he could have been by means of divine
grace, which never fails, Christ would have illuminated him;
because as the true and divine Christ alone was born and
lived for all, so also did he die for all. He looked upon

the good thief with the eyes of his mercy, also maybe
with his bodily eyes as he had looked upon Peter. The good
thief was also a symbol of the elect who shall be at the
right side and enter paradise, not through their merits,
but those of Jesus Christ; the wicked at the left side will
damn themselves through their misdeeds. [He was also a
sign] that nobody should have to despair, seeing that in
the end such a great thief was saved, who even after he was
on the cross truly spoke to Christ, as one can read in Matt.
27. Thus he stood in the place of all the elect saved only
through the goodness, kindness, and mercy of God.

Was it not a great event that on that Good Friday, when
the doors to divine treasures were opened, and when Christ
was shedding his blood with such fervor, causing by his
wounds the grape juice of divine love to overflow[4] and
showering down graces in such abundance, a thief was
illuminated and saved? Oh, how great were his faith, hope,
and love! He offered to Christ his heart and all his love,
his thoughts, his tongue and words, and more, he offered
himself entire hanging on the cross, first confessing his
sins, and not only his but those of all sinners whom he
represented. Yet, as we read in St. Luke, chapter 23, he
said: "We are suffering justly, receiving according to our
deeds,[5] and therefore endure it." Sinners, because they
think they are right, all do the opposite and say with the
bad thief: "If you are Christ (for they doubt him), save
yourself and us."[6] They do not want to suffer what is
coming to them, but say: "What good is it to pray to your
Father? If you are Christ, save yourself and us," as if
saying: "You are not Christ; therefore you do not save
yourself." The wicked are worse the more they suffer, but
the good open their eyes through chastisement and recognize Christ, as the good thief did on the cross. He, in
confessing his sins, admitted that he suffered justly
and excused the innocent Christ, saying: "This man has
not sinned and suffers for us and for our faults,

constrained only by his goodness and excessive love. We
should show compassion and gratitude toward him, since
he suffers for us and not for himself, and praying for
us he excuses us." And he reproved the bad thief, saying:
"You don't even fear God, yet are on the cross and close
to death." Then he said, praying: "Christ, Lord, remember
me when you are in your kingdom!" Here he confesses
Christ's divinity, calling him "Lord"; here is faith full of
divine wisdom; he did not ask for transient, but divine
things: only that he should remember him. Here was profound humility, as if he said: "I do not deserve to be in
heaven near you with other saints, nor to live in paradise
with the blessed; grant at least that I live in your remembrance; it will suffice me, although I shall be damned, that
you sometimes remember me. When I know this, I shall consider myself blessed although suffering eternal punishment."
Oh what great fortitude and steadfastness; when hanging on
the cross in such torment, he rose above himself remembering
only Christ, and with such moderation resigned himself to
the divine will, distributing everything with perfect
justice: to God glory and honor, to himself shame and
punishment, and to the bad thief destruction. Therefore
Christ answered him so kindly: "Verily I say to you that
today you shall be in paradise with me."[7] Not only did
he promise him paradise, but that the promise might be
really firm he added "verily," as if saying: "Be certain,
do not doubt, although you were a wicked person and a thief
and saw me suffer so much on the cross; today we will
definitely be together in paradise." Consider the great
present which he made him. He asked to be remembered, and
Christ promised him paradise. And when? That same day.
And with whom? With Christ. Oh what company! And for
how long? Forever. And to whom did he promise such
blessing? To a most vile thief, who was on the cross because of his faults, and who was cursing him a short while
before. And why did Christ promise him paradise? Because
the thief asked him to remember him.

Woman: I am certain that he is in paradise, because
Christ has said so; I think that he is a great saint,
receiving many favors.

Man: First of all, he alone among all the elect
deserved to suffer together with Christ the punishment of
the cross and to keep him company; he alone in his heart
joined Mary in having faith in Christ and compassion with
him. On that day when the others were fleeing, he alone
on the gibbet of the cross fearlessly proclaimed publicly
the innocence and divinity of Christ and reproved the
other thief and maybe other Jews [as well]. I believe that
he also said compassionate words to Mary, even though they
are not written down by the evangelists. Imagine how Mary
accepted him with Saint John as her son,[8] when she heard
that he would be with Christ in paradise on that same day;
she considered him happy above the other elect, since he
asked for grace when Christ was dispensing it to all, and
in dying was giving it to all. Therefore we must believe
that he received an abundance of grace, especially since
on his side the sacred side of Christ was opened; thence he
stood in place of all the elect. For these reasons I
believe that he is in glory at Christ's side, just as he
had been on the cross. It would not be possible to do a
more welcome deed for a king, if he were accused and
calumniated by all of his men, than for one person to excuse
and defend him and be a witness to his innocence and goodness, as the thief did for Christ. In our tribulations we
can learn from him to say: "We suffer justly according to
our deserts. Christ alone suffered unjustly."

The thief wanted to say: "I have read of Abel and Cain
who were brothers, and one was pleasing to God while the
other was not; indeed, the latter despaired." Hanging on
the cross with the other thief, the first did not want to
despair, but said to himself: "Maybe I will be forgiven.
I have also read about Noah, who was tricked by his son
Cham and covered by Sem. Therefore the one was cursed and
the other blessed by him.[9] It is my task to excuse you;
maybe you will bless me. Abraham also had two sons, one by

a free woman, the other by a slave. If my fellow-thief
wants to be the son of the synagogue and have the spirit
of fear and bondage, and thus be unwilling to suffer,
I want to strive to become the first son of your holy
church, your new bride, and have the spirit of love as
good sons do. Isaac had two sons, Jacob and Esau, one of
whom made fun of his inheritance, while the other sought
it. Thus if my fellow-thief does not care about heaven,
I will endeavor to possess it." He also wanted to say:
"When you are in your kingdom, where you are the rightful
heir to the inheritance acquired for us by your precious
blood, remember me. I am not saying, when you are great in
this life, since your kingdom is not of this world, but
when you are in your heavenly kingdom. Do not remember my
sins, my errors, my wretchedness, the thefts I have committed, but remember that I am a weak and base man, and
your creature in your image and likeness, made by you for
eternal happiness. Remember that for me you created everything, for me you took on human nature, for me you preached,
fasted, prayed, slept on the ground, wearied yourself, and
suffered for thirty-three years. Remember that I am your
kinsman and that you are dying for me. I am not asking for
great things because I am not worthy of them; I am ashamed
to ask you to bring to paradise as great a scoundrel as
me. I realize that it is not the place for me and that you
have a thousand reasons for not wanting me there. I am not
asking to be in heaven to serve those that are in paradise;
I don't deserve that. I am only asking to remain in your
memory. Do not forget those for whom you are shedding so
much blood and for whom you suffer so much, those who are
your companions on the cross. Do not consider my malice,
but rather your perfect goodness, from where the doors to
your treasures open. Although hoping to obtain grace, I
beg for charity, and if possible I would like to steal
paradise in my last hour, just as in my life I have been
a thief of earthly things. I heard you praying to the
Father for those who nailed you on the cross, excusing them

with such gentleness by saying that they do not know what
they are doing; therefore you must not be surprised if I
dare to ask you. I have seen you declare your mother to
be the mother of all sinners, so that burning with love
they may yearn for salvation; therefore I have confidence
to ask you. I am on the cross, as you see, but have three
crosses in my heart more bitter than this one: the first
of sorrow, because my fellow-thief does not repent, the
second of the fear of hell that I see, and the third of
compassion for you and your mother. Still, with all this,
my crosses would be sweet to me if I knew that you would
remember me in paradise."

Then Christ answered: "Today is that day of eternity,
when there is neither past nor future, but when everything
is the present. We still are subject to time, but you
shall be with me in paradise, because you shall see my
divine essence, my emptying Limbo of all the saints of
the Old Testament, and the skies opening. You shall ascend
with me to the empyrean heaven with the other saints, and
there always enjoy my presence in triumph and glory."

Christ wanted us in his absence to use kind words to
the sick and those who are close to death. He began to
give the daily wage to the last first, in St. Matt. 20, 8,
starting with the thief. To the first thief he said: "You
are dust, and to dust you shall return".[10] To the last of
the Old Testament he said: "Today you shall be in paradise
with me."[11] That thief is truly in paradise; I know that
he is on the cross for Christ, suffering only for his love
at the point of death.

We also, like Christ, will be on the cross through the
pains of death and between two thieves, namely the good and
bad angel, and frequently also our relatives who stand
around like true thieves in order to get our possessions,
but do not care about our souls. Therefore it is better to
dispense [with possessions] and to prepare oneself, since
it is a great thing to be able to get ready for death.
Just as the conversion of the thief was the last miracle

Christ performed, so it was the greatest of all. Thus
Your Excellency[12] must not hesitate or despair if you
should find yourself in a similar situation. Following
the example of the good thief, always seek to live mindful
not of earthly persons, who will forget you, and which
would profit you little, but seek to live happily, mindful
of Christ through love and virtue. Christ in his glory
cannot forget us if we always remember his bitter passion.

4. A Letter of Marcantonio Flaminio
to Teodorina Sauli (1542)

A. Introduction

The poet Marcantonio Flaminio was born in 1498 in Vittorio Veneto (then called Serravalle), near Treviso. He received a careful education from his father Giovanni Antonio, a humanist teacher and writer of some reputation. Flaminio was sent to Rome in 1514 for further study; his attractive personality facilitated his acquaintance with humanists and officials at the court of Pope Leo X, where he was soon admired for his Latin poetry.

Flaminio began following a pattern of life which he later modified but never abandoned: he became attached to a succession of patrons of humanists in whose households he lived for a shorter or longer time and with whom he formed genuine friendships. The first of his patrons was Baldassare Castiglione, whom he accompanied to Urbino for several months in 1515, before attending the University of Padua, where he lived in the household of the Genoese nobleman Stefano Sauli, an apostolic protonotary and a great friend of poets and writers, as well as the founder of a short-lived literary academy. He accompanied Sauli to Genoa in 1521 and to Rome the following year. There he met Gianmatteo Giberti, the papal datary, and became a member of his household in 1524. When Giberti left Rome for his bishopric of Verona after the sack of 1527, Flaminio accompanied him and remained his secretary for ten years. Giberti was a zealous prelate, deeply concerned with church reform. Through him Flaminio met like-minded churchmen such as Gasparo Contarini, the Benedictine Gregorio Cortese, and Reginald Pole, who lived in Italy in exile because of his unwillingness to accept the religious policies of his cousin, King Henry VIII.

Flaminio received three benefices between 1536 and 1538,

and with them financial independence. For reasons of
health he travelled to Naples, where around 1539 an important event in his life occurred: the meeting with Juan de
Valdés[1] and acceptance into his circle.

Valdés and his brother Alfonso were members of an old
Spanish family. Both were suspected of heresy by the Spanish
inquisition. Alfonso became one of Charles V's secretaries,
while Juan left Spain for imperial and then papal employ-
ment in Italy and in 1534 or 1535 settled in Naples. He
became the spiritual guide of a group which met at his
house for scriptural reading, prayer, and discussion. It
was composed of laymen and noble ladies, who sought a personal, vital form of Christianity and were concerned above
all with the nature of Christian life in the world. In his
works Valdés placed little emphasis on the structure or
doctrines of the Roman church. He did not attack them;
they simply were not major problems for his thought. His
foci were the human experience of God's forgiveness and
love and the dynamic nature of the relationship between
the justified Christian and God. Valdés came close to
many key Protestant concepts, especially justification by
faith. Over and over again he dwelled on the benefits of
Christ's death for the Christian and the regeneration of
his nature so that it would become capable of answering God
through an ever deepening spiritual union with him.

Flaminio was deeply influenced by Valdés's religious
ideas and emphases. Until the end of his life he devoted
himself to scriptural study. His reading included works by
Protestant authors, and his friends men such as Bernardino
Ochino and Peter Martyr Vermigli, who fled Italy to Geneva
in 1542, or Pietro Carnesecchi, burned as a heretic in
1567.[2] But Cardinal Pole also was his close friend; upon
becoming papal legate in Viterbo in 1541, he invited
Flaminio to come and stay with him. Flaminio lived in

the cardinal's household, accompanied him to the first
session of the Council of Trent in 1545, and died in Pole's
house in Rome on February 17, 1550.[3]

Flaminio's letter to Teodorina Sauli, a relative of
Stefano Sauli, his former patron, is a good example of his
spirituality. Reminiscent of Valdés even in its phrasing,[4]
the letter shows how far Flaminio's conception of the
Christian life was removed from an institutional framework.
Yet he died after receiving the sacraments of the Catholic
church, with Cardinal Carafa, the future Pope Paul IV, at
his bedside. Carafa and Flaminio had been members of the
Roman Oratory of Divine Love in 1524;[5] the stern prelate more than observed its rule concerning spiritual help
to the sick by inquiring into Flaminio's faith and presum-
ably satisfying himself about his orthodoxy.

The question of whether Flaminio was a Catholic
or at least in his sympathies a Protestant has been
answered differently by those who looked to his writings
alone and those who considered the manner of his death, or
the trust placed in him by men like Giberti or Pole (although the latter himself became suspect to the inquisition
before being vindicated).[6] Maybe Flaminio is best approach-
ed as an example of a gentle, sincere Christian for whom the
problems of man's inner reform, relation to God, and the
nature of Christian life were central. He was influenced
by Protestant reformers and their teachings on justification, and seems to have read Calvin's *Institutes* as early
as 1540 or 1541. But a clear formulation of the doctrine
of justification by the Catholic church did not exist until
the first session of the Council of Trent. It would be
difficult to imagine how someone of Flaminio's serious
interest in reform could fail to think about ideas of the
northern reformers. Only gradually did the lines separating
Protestant from Catholic theology become tightly drawn.
This did not happen until the latter part of Flaminio's

life. For him, there were alternatives in areas where
eventually none would exist.

There is no satisfactory critical modern biography of
Flaminio. The most recent work by Carol Maddison,
Marcantonio Flaminio, Poet, Humanist and Reformer (London:
Routledge and Kegan Paul, 1965), remains fragmentary and
does not supersede the older book by Ercole Cuccoli, *M.
Antonio Flaminio* (Bologna: N. Zanichelli, 1897). The
following is helpful: Giuseppe Biadego, "Marcantonio
Flaminio ai servigi di Gianmatteo Giberti vescovo di
Verona," *Atti del R. Istituto di Scienze, Lettere ed Arti*,
LXV (1905-6), pp. 209-228. Many references to Flaminio were
made by his friend Pietro Carnesecchi during his trial by
the Roman inquisition in 1566-67; see Giacomo Manzoni, ed.,
"Estratto del Processo di Pietro Carnesecchi," *Miscellanea
di Storia Italiana*, X (1870), pp. 187-573, reprinted in
Oddone Ortolani, *Per la Storia della vita religiosa italiana
nel Cinquecento, Pietro Carnesecchi* (Florence: Le Monnier,
1963), pp. 171-260.

The following letter is translated from: Giuseppe
Paladino, ed., *Opuscoli e lettere di riformatori italiani
del Cinquecento*, I (Bari: Laterza, 1913), pp. 68-71.

B. Text
Marcantonio Flaminio to Teodorina Sauli
Naples, 12 February (1542)

The affection which I have for Your Ladyship because of
the love you bear to Jesus Christ our Lord made me write
you what I did. But if I was presumptuous and arrogant,
Your Ladyship is all the more humble and modest, asking me
in your letter to teach you how to build on the foundation
set forth in my last one. Although I know that I would do
better to imitate your humility and keep silent, nevertheless, in obedience to your wishes, I shall recommend

briefly three things, which I know from experience to be
most helpful for the strengthening of spiritual life. They
are: mental prayer, Christian adoration, and meditation.

By mental prayer I mean a fervent desire to obtain
something from God; and the things that we should wish to
obtain from God above all others are faith, hope, and
charity. Because man is always capable of desire, he can
also always pray, as St. Paul exhorts us to do.[7] Christian
faith consists in believing all the words of God, especially
the Gospel of Christ. The Gospel is nothing but the joyful
message which the apostles proclaimed throughout the whole
world; they affirmed that the only-begotten Son of God,
having assumed our flesh, has given satisfaction to his
eternal Father's justice for all our sins. Whoever believes
the glad tidings, believes the Gospel, and believing the
Gospel through the grace of God, leaves the kingdom of
this world to enter the kingdom of God, enjoying the
general pardon. From a carnal creature, he becomes a
spiritual one; from a child of wrath, a child of grace;
from the son of Adam, the son of God. Guided by the Holy
Spirit, he feels a joyous peace of conscience. He strives
to mortify the affections and desires of the flesh, knowing
that he is dead with his head, Jesus Christ. He also
strives to revive the spirit, and to lead a heavenly life
in the knowledge of his resurrection with the same Jesus
Christ.[8] These and other marvellous results are brought
about by living faith in the soul of the Christian. Therefore we must always persist in praying to God to give it to
us and to increase it, if we already have it.

Christian hope consists in patient expectation, with
desire and unceasing joy, that God will fulfill in us the
promises he made to all the members of his beloved Son.
He promised to make us conform to his glorious likeness.
This will be fulfilled when, after the resurrection of the
just, we shall be glorified, body and soul. Whoever
possesses this hope always cries with his whole heart: "Thy
kingdom come!" This kingdom will truly come when Jesus

Christ delivers it to his eternal Father after the last
judgment.

Charity consists in loving God for himself and everything for God, and in directing all of one's thoughts,
words, and deeds to the glory of his divine majesty. This
can never be done by someone who does not believe in the
Gospel and anticipate through hope the riches of eternal
life. Thus the Christian must live with a continuous
desire that God might increase his faith by which he knows
himself justified and made a son of God through the merits
of Christ; that God might increase his hope, through which
he awaits with longing the resurrection of the just; and
that God might increase his charity, through which he
loves God with his whole heart, hating self-love, the
source of all sin.

Charity sustains faith and hope because it makes man
believe and hope easily. Hope of eternal life makes the
Christian not anxious about the present life, and as a
result he is modest and humble in prosperity and strong
and patient in adversity. Living faith keeps us joined to
Christ and thus vivified by the spirit of Christ, which is
most bountiful. It produces the sweetest fruits in the
soul of the true Christian, such as charity, joy, peace,
kindness, goodness, meekness, fidelity, and hope. I firmly
believe that the soul that feels itself to be completely
without these and similar heavenly fruits does not have
within itself the spirit of Christ; and he who does not
have the spirit of Christ is not of Christ, as St. Paul
says.[9]

Christian adoration consists of the spirit and the
truth. Thus the Christian worships in spirit and truth when
he humiliates himself under the powerful hand of God,
praising his holy name at all times and giving thanks for
everything, bad fortune as well as good. He firmly believes
that nothing happens to him without the will of God. In
making his own will conform to God's, the Christian becomes
united with God and one in spirit with him. He enjoys a

most tranquil peace and is safe from all tumults and errors
of the world. Therefore, even if infirmity, persecution,
poverty, death of his children, and all other kinds of
adversity were to befall him, he should accept them with
a joyful and serene face, in the knowledge that they come
through the will of God. The Christian has made that will
his own; he desires all that God wills, who purifies the
souls of his elect in the furnace of tribulations, leading
them to the happiness of paradise along the very same way
that was taken by his only-begotten son, Jesus Christ.

Meditation consists in thinking of God, his perfection,
and the benefits liberally bestowed by his omnipotence,
wisdom, and infinite goodness on all creatures, but
especially on true Christians. It also consists in thinking of Jesus Christ in his corporeal and mortal state and
of Jesus Christ resurrected and immortal. The Christian
should meditate on the humility, meekness, charity,
obedience to God, and extreme poverty of the corporeal and
mortal Jesus Christ, and the continuous ignominy and persecutions which finally led to his most bitter death on the
wood of the cross. Let the true Christian think about
these things every day in order to imitate his master, to
become humble, meek, loving, obedient to God, to overcome
the shame of this world, to be patient and constant in
tribulation, to take up his cross every day and follow his
master intrepidly.

Thinking of Jesus Christ impassible, immortal, and
glorified, the Christian should consider that he has been
exalted by God to the loftiest heights because of his
obedience, acquiring a name which is above any other name.
Let the Christian consider that he is our high priest because he always intercedes for us; our Lord, since he has
saved and redeemed us by his most precious blood; our
king, since he guides us with his Holy Spirit, in temporal
as well as spiritual matters; our head, since, as from a
man's head there proceeds a force which gives life and
feeling to the whole body, so from our glorious Christ

there proceeds to his mystical members a divine power,
giving them eternal life and richly endowing them with
heavenly and spiritual gifts and sentiments. The Christian
should consider that Christ loves us infinitely and cares
for us more than we ourselves do; that with his purity and
perfection he covers all our imperfections and dwells in
our souls with his spirit; and, finally, that he will make
us live with him in paradise, rejoicing in the likeness of
his glory.

Who, meditating on these marvellous things with faith,
would not be consumed with divine love? Or would not come
to love God and Jesus Christ most ardently? Or would not
judge and consider all the honors, riches, satisfactions,
and pleasures of the world to be nothing but vile filth?
Or refuse to consecrate his soul and body to his God and
to Christ?

My Lady, always think of God and Christ. Then you will
live a heavenly life on earth, seeing God and Christ in
everything, doing all things for their glory, and loving
everything for the love of God and Christ. My dearest Lady
in Christ, in order to obey you I have been presumptuous,
speaking of spiritual matters, in which I know myself to
be but an amateur. Yet bear with my mistakes this time.
In the future seek out persons qualified for such a task
and leave me to be silent. Only pray to God to make me
hear what he speaks to my heart in secret. I beseech God
always to make you pray, adore him, and meditate to his
honor and glory.

II. The Question of Institutional Reform

5. Gianpietro Carafa, *Memorial*
to Pope Clement VII (1532)

A. Introduction

Gianpietro Carafa was born in 1476 into a noble family
of the Kingdom of Naples. He received a good part of his
education in the household of his uncle, Cardinal Oliviero
Carafa, and was ordained a priest. His rise to prominence
was rapid: he became bishop of Chieti in the Abruzzi in 1505,
papal nunzio to England in 1513 and to Spain in 1515, and
archbishop of Brindisi in 1518. Soon he gained a reputation
as a strong-minded and zealous reforming churchman. Re-
nouncing his ecclesiastical dignities, in 1524 together with
St. Gaetano da Thiene he founded the Theatine Order. Unlike
older monastic orders, Theatines had no distinctive habit or
choir prayer; rather, they devoted themselves to the cure of
souls and practical works of charity, especially among
the sick and poor. When the troops of Charles V sacked Rome
in 1527, Carafa together with a small group of Theatines fled
to Venice, where he chiefly resided until 1536, when he was
made a Cardinal by Pope Paul III.

Between 1536 and 1555 he followed a distinguished
curial career and participated in the work of several
commissions on church reform. Cardinal Carafa was known as
an intransigent opponent of Protestantism. A member of the
Roman Inquisition from its founding in 1542, he was committed
to the extirpation of heresy, and advocated strict means
of controlling the spread of heterodox ideas. As Pope Paul
IV from 1555 to 1559 he attempted to put his conception of
rigorous church reform into practice. One example is the
Index of Prohibited Books of 1559.

The violence of his temperament, excessive suspicion
of anyone he considered leaning toward heresy, unfortunate
family entanglements, and ill-considered anti-Spanish political manoeuvres combined to make him feared and hated. His

death was followed by a destructive popular riot in Rome and
other places of the papal state. He is remembered as the
most intransigent of the Counter-Reformation popes, and has
found little sympathy among later historians.

The memorial instructing the Franciscan friar Bonaventura about matters to be brought to the pope's attention
was written in 1532, when Carafa was living in Venice. It
is a typical example of his views on the causes of abuses
in the church and the measures necessary to correct them.
But more than one man's opinions, the memorial represents
a particular concept of reform which saw discipline, rather
than the resolution of theological issues or individual
religious commitment, as the central element in any revitali-
zation of the church. To Carafa the chief evils besetting
the church were due to the laxity of regular and secular
religious superiors, the corruption of curial officials and
offices, above all the Penitentiary, and the pope's lack of
firmness in dealing with heretics and those guilty of abuses.

There is no hint of accommodation with new ideas in the
memorial. For Carafa, the tightening of discipline, observance of already existing laws and regulations, and repres-
sive measures against those who do not heed them or who
spread heresy are necessary to insure the welfare of the
church and the Christian people.

Thus his memorial represents an unusually clear
example of reform seen as a purely ecclesiastical matter,
an institutional house-cleaning operation, as it were. While
written with passion and even excessive bluntness, it is also
curiously one-dimensional, and shows no awareness of the
range of religious problems agitating his contemporaries.

The literature dealing with Gianpietro Carafa is not
extensive. No up-to-date biography of him exists. An
old but informative life written by Antonio Caracciolo, a
Neapolitan Theatine of the seventeenth century, has never
been printed in its entirety, and exists in manuscript versions, including one in the Newberry Library in Chicago.
Useful are: Ludwig von Pastor, *History of the Popes*, Vol.

XIV (St. Louis: Herder, 1924), 56-424; G. M. Monti, *Ricerche su papa Paolo IV Carafa* (Benevento: Cooperativa tipografia chiostro S. Sofia, 1925); H. Jedin, "Analekten zur Reformtätigkeit der Päpste Julius III. und Paul IV.," *Römische Quartalschrift*, 42 (1934), pp. 305-22 and 43 (1935), pp. 87-156.

The text of the memorial is translated from Ioannes Petrus Carafa, "De Lutheranorum haeresi reprimenda et ecclesia reformanda ad Clementem VII [4. octobris 1532]," in *Concilium Tridentinum. Diariorum Actorum Epistularum Tractatuum nova collectio*. Ed. Societas Goerresiana, Vol. XII (Freiburg im Breisgau: Herder, 1929), pp. 67-77.

B. Text

Information Sent to Pope Clement VII
by the Bishop of Chieti through
Brother Bonaventura of the Franciscan Order
[October 4, 1532]

Reverend Father.[1] With the grace of God and in obedience to your superiors you are going to Rome, where you will visit the church of the Prince of the Apostles, perform your devotions, and pray for me. Give my letter to Master Francesco Vanucio, canon of S. Maria in Trastevere and director of the hospital for incurables; you will find him there. Then, when he has an opportunity to conduct you into the presence of His Holiness, whose feet you will humbly kiss, recommend me to him, asking his blessing on me, and thank him warmly for the gracious favor granted to the convent of my sister in Naples.[2]

Afterward tell His Holiness that you should have been sent to him long ago and that it is necessary for you to be given a favorable and undisturbed audience, since it does not happen very frequently that such trustworthy messengers can be sent to him, and writing is dangerous. Since this city [Venice] is neither the smallest nor the most despicable place in Christendom, and since in it and its territory

are many thousands of souls committed to [the care of] His
Holiness, beg him to listen for the sake of God's honor and
his own to a trustworthy person telling something of what
ought to be done for them. Although [the subject of] their
needs is a broad one, yet some of its aspects will be considered now. Because, as the apostle says, it is impossible
to please God without faith,[3] begin with this topic and tell
His Holiness what people think about the errors and heresies
in the lives and behavior of some who do not observe Lent
or go to confession, and so on, and in the beliefs of others
who hold these errors, discuss them publicly, and still read
prohibited books without concern. Above all, report that
the infection of Lutheran heresy as well as every other
error against faith and good practices is being disseminated
most effectively and made to increase by two kinds of people,
namely apostates and conventual friars.[4] His Holiness should
know about this accursed nest of conventual Franciscan
friars, which God in his goodness has begun to confound by
the hand of some of his servants. Since [these friars] were
disciples of a heretical friar who recently died, they want
to do honor to the master, and all are heretics. One of
them is Galateo,[5] whose affair His Holiness committed to my
care two years ago, and having found him to be a relapsed
and incorrigible heretic, I condemned him. He is still
imprisoned, and the judgment against him has not been executed because they [the Venetian government] excuse themselves by saying that His Holiness has not yet made any
move against his heresies and that they consider themselves
not obliged to do more than the pope in such matters. Although they don't deny their intention of executing the sentence, they have deferred doing it until now.

     The other fellow-disciple of the above-mentioned
[Galateo] is Friar Bartholomeo[6] of the same order, who was
suspended from preaching in S. Hieremia two years ago by the
papal legate, the bishop of Pola[7] of blessed memory, because
of heresy. Seeing himself prevented from going about in-
fecting and corrupting the poor souls in this land, he went

to Augsburg, cast off the [monastic] habit, and now lives
as a Lutheran. Being the evil person he is, he dared to
boast of frightening the Pope, especially since it is
rumored that His Holiness has ordered Jacopo Salviati[8] to
write him. It is also said that His Holiness has written
him a brief of some sort, which causes extreme pain to
every good and faithful Christian who sees that, if His
Holiness has done this, he was very badly served by those
who should have made him understand the truth, which is that
heretics must be treated as heretics. Lowering himself by
writing to them or by speaking gently and permitting certain
favors for them to be extorted from His Holiness could
accidentally succeed in [returning] one of them [to the
fold]; but ordinarily this is the way to make heretics grow
more obdurate and to increase their number daily. Already
the evildoers boast that this is the way to be honored,
appointed to office, and beneficed by His Holiness, which is
most shameful and dangerous.

     Another fellow-disciple is Friar Alexander of Pieve
di Sacco,[9] who was seized by the ordinary of Padua because
of the many heresies he has spread about. Although he is
still in prison, I hear that the case against him is prose-
cuted without zeal. Although more people belonging to
several orders were among the suspect, still their leader
(or, rather, their general) seems to be this arch-heretic,
who, as you know, went around spreading poison everywhere.
In this region and particular city of such great importance
[Padua] he has lit so big a fire that, if God sends no
remedy through his mercy, some day His Holiness could grieve
and repent of the immunity which is said to have been granted
[to Friar Alexander] and of so many briefs and favors which
the latter boasts of having received from His Holiness. Urge
His Holiness not to think that his briefs and kindnesses
toward a hardened heretic like this can have any other effect
than to make him more resourceful and insidious, and consequently more harmful to the church. He will become obstinate
and perfidious, hurt the reputation of His Holiness, and

demoralize and sadden the minds of faithful Christians who
see themselves offended by evildoers in the guise of sheep
under protection of the authority of the Apostolic See. By
the love of God, beseech His Holiness to curb his officials
from issuing such an abundance of apostolic briefs for every
insignificant and tangential matter.

II

Several times the chancellor has admonished his master,
who does not want to come to his senses.[10] There are similar
insistent complaints about some others, and no remedy is in
sight. In general, I conclude by saying that His Holiness
must provide a remedy both for the honor of God and because
of the duties attached to his office, in order to be able
to render an accounting to God. It occurs to me in this
context that in a time of such urgency one cannot proceed
as if it were business as usual, but just as in the growing
furor of war, every day new and appropriate provisions have
to be made, so in the greater spiritual war one must not
remain asleep. As His Holiness knows, the office of the inquisition in this province is in the hands of the above-
mentioned conventual Franciscans, who by chance happened to
appoint a suitable inquisitor, such as Master Martin of
Treviso,[11] of whose diligence and faith I know His Holiness
to have been informed by the already mentioned Bishop of
Pola of blessed memory. [Because Master Martin] has left
that office for another, he was succeeded as inquisitor by
someone I don't know, who, as I hear, is quite inept. Therefore it is necessary that His Holiness should first make
provisions to shake up the ordinaries, because they are almost everywhere asleep, and then depute some persons with
authority and send here a [papal] legate, who, if possible,
is neither ambitious not grasping, and who will see to it
that the honor and credit of the Holy Apostolic See are
re-established. He should punish or at least put to flight
the wicked heretics in the midst of poor Christians, since
wherever they go they will carry with them the testimony of

their own iniquity and of the goodness of the Catholic
faithful, who do not want them in their midst.

III

Since the pestilence of heresy is usually introduced
either through sermons and heretical books or through long
habituation to an evil and dissolute life, from which it is
easy to move to heresy, it seems that His Holiness could
make a holy, good, and useful provision in this matter,
which I remember having previously mentioned to him three
or four years ago. It is this: let His Holiness order
the patriarch[12] here, and elsewhere the other bishops, to
whom approved persons belonging to monastic orders are
joined, together to examine diligently all those who have
to be appointed to preach or hear confessions and to gather
information not only about their adequacy and goodness, but
above all about their way of life, reputation, and Catholic
belief. Only those that are approved and expressly given
permission by them should be permitted to exercise the above-
mentioned functions, and no others. For this examination
or permission no money or other imposition should be required. If perhaps those who do not have a spiritual but only
a material outlook should oppose His Holiness so as to prevent this great good, certainly His Holiness should silence
them, since indeed they do not know what they are saying.
[These same people argue that] the privileges granted to
religious orders should not be revoked by the measures taken
by His Holiness on account of the urgent necessity which
exists. They [further] say that the superiors of religious
orders can conduct the examinations. Oh, what a fine way of
doing things! Blessed is he who [is foolish enough to] hope
for it! You can inform His Holiness of the truth which you
know about all this. Maybe some men who are timid where
there should be no fear will argue that wayward and incapable
friars, finding themselves suspended from preaching and
hearing confessions, which are the means of gaining their
livelihood, will then fall into despair and become apostates

and heretics. I cannot answer such a vile and unworthy, not to say most stupid notion because of the strong
nausea [I feel]; certainly using this same reasoning, or
rather, totally irrational vileness, it would be necessary
to give up on infinite [numbers] of other pastoral offices.
Still, there might be another [kind of] opposition which
would not seem so reprehensible, by those who say that as a
result of the above provision only a small number of
approved preachers and confessors would remain. May God
grant that there be not so many, provided they are good
ones! Yet I do not intend to suggest that the examiners
appointed by His Holiness should pursue matters so minutely
as to be dissatisfied with all those who should be allowed
to remain in their jobs, provided they are Catholic and
averagely suited to their office. The result will be that
immediately the spirit of the entire good and faithful
people will be miraculously comforted, because it will
appear to them that His Holiness truly keeps watch over his
flock, that the heretics have nothing to murmur about, and
that all friars of whatever sort will make an effort to
bring order into their lives and beliefs, so as not to be
reproved. The effect [of this provision] will be most
fruitful.

        Leaving aside [a discussion of] the importance of
preachers as a most obvious subject, that of confessors is
not only not smaller but much greater, since it is more
hidden and common and the evil [done] by them can be felt or
seen only later on. Every insignificant and vile person
sets himself up [as a confessor]. Not by way of a story or
hyperbole, but in an insistent manner I have been repeatedly
told that in several monasteries of conventuals some friars
who are not priests at times set themselves up to hear confessions, in order to rob a few pennies. I will be silent
about the scandals of revealing confessions and granting
dispensations to remain in mortal sin and in all sorts of
papal excommunications, which now have come to be disdained
and derided with contempt only on account of the confessors.

IV

His Holiness should know that in this state [Venice] the majority of important people do not go to confession and communion each year. If they are sometimes admonished by conscientious and anxious friends, they openly excuse themselves by saying that their confessors give them permission to do certain things which they know they should not do as good Christians. Once again, in the interest of decency, I will say nothing about the obscenity of some vicious confessors, because of whom the name of the Lord is blasphemed.[13] I conclude that evil living and corrupt morals thrive only because of wicked confessors. Get His Holiness to understand that this matter of confessors is more important than I can possibly express. He must be moved to pity toward so many souls, be mindful of the honor of God as well as of his own, and provide a remedy because it is so easy and simple for him to do it, while its benefit is so certain and great.

V

Since mention of apostates has already been made above, His Holiness should know that however [bad] they may have been in times past (one always reads that they were most wicked; St. Augustine swears that he has not seen worse men than they are), today we see that all those who leave their orders also become apostates from the faith, so that there are no worse founders, defenders, and sowers of heresy than they. Some go about in the habit of secular priests; others are dressed like laymen; they penetrate into private houses and infect convents of nuns and other places. Because of the liberality of the church there are many children and even some soldiers who each possess at least three or four parish churches. In order to profit from them [financially] as much as they can, they try to have few expenses. It seems to the holders of benefices that they can not find more suitable curates to take their place than the above apostates. They do not appoint other chaplains to their parishes than those cursed

apostates, who enter the churches like wolves. They take
upon themselves the cure of souls, making a mockery of
Christ's blood and of his holy faith, a business of the
sacraments in which they do not believe, and of the poor
souls such that no tongue can [adequately] express it.
Although they have shed the habits of their orders as well
as their faith, nevertheless because of their long stay in
monasteries they retain a certain decorum in external
actions, some knowledge of ecclesiastical ceremonies, and in
some cases, of letters. In part because of their hypocrisy
and ostentation and in part on account of the attraction and
curious nature of various heresies which please many because
of their novelty and licentiousness, these apostates are
followed by the common multitide with great sympathy. I
call "common multitude" all those who favor them; because
of our sins there are those among them whom the world does
not consider as part of the vulgar crowd [i.e. members of
the upper classes].

Since the number of these abominable apostates by now
has increased to such an extent that someone trying to think
of a remedy is confounded, it would seem that the Pope at
least cannot excuse himself if he makes no provision for the
future. Beg His Holiness for the honor of God, the salvation
of Christendom, and in the first place for [the sake of]
his own salvation and honor to curb the mad dogs of the
Penitentiary,[14] so that their profits do not cost the
afflicted Christian commonwealth and the soul of His Holiness
such a high price. If it were lawful and honest, doubtless
a tax could be imposed on all faithful Christians, who would
gladly pay it so that an end could now be put to so many
manifest abominations. [For example,] a man who had been a
professed friar in an established order and a priest for a
good many years, with various offices and responsibilities
in his monastery for ten and sometimes for twenty years, is
enticed from the monastery by the devil and his servants.
He goes about in secular clothing. When asked why, he says
that the Penitentiary has given him a dispensation.

He shows bulls which state that he was forced into the
monastery as a minor, that he never had a commitment to
remain there, that he contracted an incurable disease, and
other similar fables. I asked such a man whether all this
was true, and he answered me that he entered [the monastery]
voluntarily when he was grown-up and healthy, that he
willingly made his profession and freely remained there.
Asked why he left, he said that some [friars] leave because
of a quarrel with other friars, some in order to escape
persecution--that is, correction by their superior. Another
will say brazenly that vows and monastic institutions are
human inventions and that he was not obliged to stay, but
in order not to be bothered by legal complications, he
procured those worthless letters from the Penitentiary,
spending money on his soul. There are still others, and
these very numerous, who obtain by fraudulent misrepresenta-
tion letters from the Penitentiary which give them permission to cast off their habit; then they don't even present
the letters, or fulfill their conditions, but instead mock
God and the Apostolic See. As mentioned above, these men
now almost everywhere have the cure of souls, and in many
places they are chaplains and confessors of nunneries.
Many conduct schools for children, while others [use their
position as] chaplains to important men in ways that enable
them to spread their poison everywhere. This [evil] cannot
be destroyed without forceful and effective help from God
and from His Holiness.

     You, my [dear] Father, could also tell His Holiness
about your monastery, and so forth, and advise him not to
accept any excuses, since the miserable apostates indeed
have told the truth of the matter. They are being ruined
by the officials of the Penitentiary with their false and
fraudulent pretenses and don't look farther [to justify]
their lack of faith and [evil] conscience, as I have
already said.

     Since we must hope that God's Majesty will inspire the

Pope sooner than others to find every remedy that is appropriate in this matter, His Holiness should realize and
remember that it is necessary for him to take action first
and beyond all others for the sake of his soul, his honor,
the state, and temporal affairs. [The dispensations
granted by the Penitentiary] together with other things
operate in favor of the Lutheran heresy, which among other
errors states that monastic vows are not valid, and so on.
Now if we grant permission so easily, without any reason
or discrimination, to all and sundry to unfrock and
apostatize, what greater aid could we give to heresy?
Therefore this worldly entrance-door [for heresy] must be
closed and bolted. His Holiness should reserve exclusively
for himself the faculty [of granting such dispensations].
In accordance with the common opinion of theologians and
canon lawyers, [this faculty] should be exercised only in
grave and important instances. In the case of those whose
vows prove not valid because of their excessive youth[15] or
some other strong legal reason, His Holiness should see to
it that their affairs are handled properly and on the basis
of actual facts by an agency other than those rapacious and
vile harpies [in the Penitentiary]. As far as the mass of
those who already have become apostates is concerned, His
Holiness should make immediate provision above all that
they can never have the cure of souls either directly in
their own persons or through [delegation to] others; [nei-
ther should they be allowed to] direct nuns, hear their
confessions, or render them other spiritual or temporal
services, much less preach or be confessors anywhere.
There should be some legal provision barring the unhappy
apostates from any [ecclesiastical] emoluments or rank in
such a way that at least the [ensuing] hardship would make
them understand the meaning [of their vows].[16] By this
action not only will such good be done to them as it is
possible to do, but also great benefits will result for
countless poor friars who are staying in monasteries like
reeds swayed by the wind because they are perturbed

and invited to become apostates when they see the great
ease with which [dispensations] are granted to all for
money. They are even further incited [to apostasy] by the
favors which they see granted by the Apostolic See and also
by the laity to the above-mentioned cursed apostates.
Since His Holiness has now appointed the head of the
Penitentiary in accordance with his own wishes,[17] he has
no excuse for not taking action in the above-mentioned
matter as well as in other needs of that office. The poor
old[18] man whom God may forgive was too comfortably settled
in his old age so that one could say of him: "Nobody puts
new wine into old wineskins";[19] rather, let us throw out
the old leaven and cast off the old man.[20]

VI

It does not behoove us who are lowly to speak of great
things because of their depth and difficulty, but only to
beseech God to help, who alone can do it. But at least
tell His Holiness this. Because of the poor quality and
greed of some of those who are supposed to be acting as
bishops, practically all cathedral churches these days are
bereft of their pastors either because they have been
given *in commendam*[21] or because these prelates are so
inflamed by ambition that they leave their churches and
hang around courts. Some of them set up in their churches
shabby friars under the appellation of titular bishops
who are called by a new name: suffragans. The term was
not used with this meaning during all past ages. Actually,
of course, suffragans are bishops belonging to the same
province, who are entitled to give their suffrages in the
election of their archbishop and therefore are called
suffragans. These friar-bishops, on the other hand, who
have come famished out of the monasteries, do not seem to
be able to get enough from the sale of sacred things to
satisfy their ravenous hunger. Because of it they help
themselves above all by selling holy orders as the most
marketable merchandise. In season and out of season they

not only admit but compel and urge all who are spiritually
and sometimes even physically blind, deaf, mute, lame, and
so on--few of the good but all of the bad--to enter through
misdeeds, namely the heresy of simony. Thus the house of
the Lord is filled with such dregs and filth that the quality of secular and now also regular priests of every order
has made the entire population disgusted with the mass,
other divine offices, and the authority and power of the
church. One can say of the people that "they have no
stomach for their food".[22] The heretics are loud in their
insults and ridicule of [these priests]; they call them
beasts, and one does not know how to answer, since the
matter is so foul that it spreads its stench everywhere.
His Holiness will remember that in the first year of his
pontificate he entrusted a loyal servant of his with the
duty of ordaining [men to the priesthood] and forbade all
others to meddle in it;[23] nevertheless there were some
bishops of the above-described kind, or similar ones, who
most shamelessly and without respect for the presence of
His Holiness went out to the street corners of Rome, ordaining as many blockheads as they could gather. Now His
Holiness can imagine how much more presumptuousness there
is in places far away from his presence. In this state
[Venice] we often hear something new about such matters,
which scandalize the whole people. Together with others,
the bishop of Veglia[24] has been mentioned in this connection; it would be better if he slept rather than watched
over such excesses as are told of him.[25] He is saying
openly and boasting that he has received from His Holiness
the privilege of ordaining everywhere, even out of season.
And so, to the great affront of God and harm to the church,
because of him and others the world is full of the sort of
priests and friars whose inability, ignorance, ineptitude,
and stupidity can neither be described nor tolerated.
Because of their great greed to transact the business of
the mass soon, we see priests who barely can be sixteen
years old. It seems certain that the enemy of God has

made use of so many gangs, most of all this one, to vex
the Christian religion and lead it to confusion and destruction (may God not permit it!).

VII

It is not necessary to say more about the habits,
tonsures, lives, and honesty [of these clerics]; there are
no ruffians or soldiers who are more dishonest, shameless,
and impudent than they, so that God's patience certainly
makes one wonder. But the patience of the world which
puts up with them seems also great. I do not know how
His Holiness can have a tranquil mind without undertaking
some measures to exonerate his conscience, even though he
may not think it will help; for without doubt it will produce great results. May His Holiness take a little heart,
and trusting in God's help, begin to do something about
this great need! Although he is busy with other matters,
he should consider that this must not be the last, since
it is not the least. His Holiness should revoke all permissions to ordain, even if they were granted either by
himself or his predecessors. He should prohibit anyone
from daring [to ordain] under the gravest penalties. As
for the multitude of those who were already promised
[ordination], let a permission be sent to the ordinary
bishops through deputies of His Holiness, as we mentioned
above, who shall also be charged with examining all
priests, admitting those suited [to the priesthood], sus-
pending the unsuitable, and informing themselves about
strangers, because among the latter are some who set a price
on the priesthood. With these provisions His Holiness will
grant a benefit to all, especially to this state, because
he will encourage the Patriarch to return and reside in his
own church from which he has long been absent, to the great
detriment of his flock and himself and the scandal and
complaint of all.[26]

Since mention has already been made of heretical books,
inform His Holiness that they are freely exhibited and owned

here by many, both friars and secular priests; some hold
[ecclesiastical] censures openly in contempt, while others
pretend to have permission to keep such books. If that
were true, [such permission] should definitely be restricted
or revoked, since we see that in many cases the possession
and reading of these books have been the ruin of their
owners and of others, not because these cursed books
contain such exquisite teaching or valid arguments so as to
produce this result, but because the persons [reading them]
are of themselves ill-disposed, readily accepting the
teachings which are in conformity with their habits and
lives. I do not see any benefit in granting permission,
except perhaps, for compelling reasons, to some outstanding
ecclesiastics whose faith, goodness, devotion, and learning
are irreproachable and clearly manifest to His Holiness.
Otherwise there is no necessity nor any benefit in granting
such permission at random to every insignificant friar, and
worse, [to satisfy the] rash and damnable curiosity of some
who are puffed up with secular learning. As for the friars
allowed to read heretical books, we see the fine result of
it: having abandoned the observances of monastic life, they
become worse than secular priests, and finally all or the
majority of those who enjoy such books fall into apostasy,
as was said above. How much better it would be for them to
attend to the right teachings of the holy fathers, through
which true faith is strengthened and right behavior learned!
I know some secular priests who told me that they have
received the said permission from His Holiness; then I,
knowing with whom I had to deal, begged them for the love
of God to take care not to avail themselves of it. They
did not listen to me. I know from experience that it would
have been better for them and for many others if they had
heeded me. I also know that I can in justice beg His
Holiness by the love of God not to grant these permissions
any more and to revoke those given because they truly are
not needed, considering that the heresies of those scoundrels are all old issues, already long ago rebutted and

wiped out by holy church, even if there were something to
discuss. Those matters which are the concern of His Holiness and not of others should be left to him [to handle]
with the sacred college or other help according to his
judgment and the nature of the issues. The Catholic faith
must not be compromised daily through entirely inept,
brawling legal quacks, who give themselves out to be the
true guardians of the church, while in fact they themselves
require a guardian.

VIII

I shall now speak about a matter of great importance,
in which I will recapitulate what was said above. Because
of it the Reverend bishop of Verona[27] and I already last
year wanted to send a message of this kind to His Holiness.
This important matter concerns the state of monastic orders,
on which the salvation or destruction of the world depends:
salvation if their condition were healthy, as when they
were founded, and ruin because they are now broken down
and deformed. Although all monastic orders are prostrate
and afflicted, nevertheless restrict yourself and speak
[only] of yours [i.e., the Observant Franciscan], since
you know it better than others, and since His Holiness
can learn about all from the example of one. Your order
alone is more important than many others to His Holiness and
the Christian community, both on account of the large number
of its members and the beautiful institution of evangelical
poverty. But, alas! Who will give my head water and my
eyes a fountain of tears?[28] Their strength is spent, those
surrounded have defected, and the remaining have dwindled.[29]
Devastated is the vineyard which formerly was set apart;
its wall is destroyed, and all who pass by rob it of its
fruit;[30] there is no cluster to eat; my soul craves the
ripe fig, but piety has perished on earth, and there is no
honesty among men.[31]

Although the wound is serious, still, with the grace
of God, the medicine is prepared, if His Holiness wants it.
Everything depends on His Holiness, if he only wants [to
act]. Feel free to tell His Holiness that I stake my
head on the following: let him make the test of investigat-
ing who the good friars in your congregation are. Although
there are [many] good ones, I speak here of those who are
good in reality, not [only] in appearance; I call them good
insofar as they are approved as being good by honest friars
in spite of evil friars and secular priests. Then let His
Holiness propose to the good friars the remedies I have
suggested. If they are not approved by them as being good,
possible, and easy, I want His Holiness to punish me not
only as a liar but as a disloyal and bad servant.

Things have come to such a pass now that His Holiness
should reflect on the burden [of responsibility] he is
carrying by not making provisions [concerning monastic
orders] and think that matters are already so bad that if
no legal measures are taken, one day the evil could give
birth to a greater monster than we can imagine. If
conventual friars whose dissolute life is known everywhere
suffice to give us such trouble as I have described in part
before, then what will those do who on the surface seem
simple and devout, if they are permitted to proceed to the
precipice toward which they are now moving? If they destroyed only themselves, the damage would be serious in any
case, but it still would be possible to have hope; but
since they are diffused in such numbers through the body of
Christendom [as to make it possible to liken them to] blood
vessels, they cannot collapse without pulling the world to
ruin with them.

IX

Now I want to speak about some more immediate remedies,
leaving the fuller or briefer discussion of others dependent
on the wishes of His Holiness. Two matters need to be dealt
with above all: first, the preservation of the entire body

of this congregation,[32] so that it does not become ruined
further. If it cannot do all the good that it might, at
least it should not do any further harm. Second, the creation of possibilities for those who want to and can do good;
they are in the minority.

   I shall briefly discuss the first matter: His Holiness
will govern the monastic orders well if he leaves them free
to convoke their chapter meetings and attend to all other
matters in accordance with their rules and constitutions.
He should not allow people to extort from him apostolic
briefs for the purpose of changing or shifting the time and
place of chapter meetings so easily, because knavish and
ambitious friars have adopted this method. When they realize that the provincial chapter meeting is fixed at an
unfavorable time for the exercise of their ambition, they
invent their own reasons and obtain briefs to hasten or
delay the chapter meeting or change it in other ways conven-
ient to themselves. Intrigues like this go on throughout
the whole province.[33] If, in order to make scheming friars
conform with their [original] purpose, and [stop] their
thwarting and tormenting of poor friars in the province and
beyond, the changing of guardians, and the banishing of good
friars from the province by appointing them preachers or
lectors [elsewhere], His Holiness wants to know about all
this and issue regulations, you can give him information
that suffices. At this point, petition His Holiness about
that which pertains to your commission regarding the provincial chapter.

   The second matter is to help those few good friars who
want to observe the strict Franciscan rule, which they have
promised to God by a solemn vow, to do so. His Holiness
cannot refuse them this, even if they did not demand it,
but rather could and perhaps should constrain them to do it.
The crowd of bad friars will say that everyone of them can
live up to his vows. I must deal with actual experience and
say that all friars, the good and the bad, admit that, at
present, in the state in which this congregation finds

itself, it is impossible, without a sweeping reformation,
to speak about, let alone observe the pure rule of St.
Francis. Since the matter is too obvious and supported
by the witness of the entire people, no [further] arguments
are necessary. If anyone says: "Well then, that entire
congregation should be reformed," I answer that this is
simply impossible for any human agency on account of the
great multitude of evil men who belong to that congregation
and keep the good oppressed in such a way that they are not
allowed to exercise any influence. The discord which arises
from the diversity of their lives and behavior is so great
that it causes enmity and parricidal hatred in the bad ones.
Thus murders happen, not only by poison, but openly by the
use of knives and swords, not to mention guns, as has been
the case in several monastic orders in these evil days. For
the good this certainly causes an anxious, painful, and
difficult life, in which they not only do not strive for
perfection, as they should, but do well indeed if they do
not look back [i.e., do not get involved with what is
happening around them].

Those who say that monastic orders will be ruined if the
good [monks] are separated [from the bad] do not understand
this matter, although they may understand others. Whoever
speaks thus about this matter shows that he does not know
why monasticism requires that its adherents live together as
one, united in their practices, as it is written about the
first and true monks: that they were of one heart and one
mind.[34] But it is too obvious that nothing good can come
from merely remaining together and that the bad not only do
not become better because of the company of the good, but as
we actually see, they become much worse almost as a retort.

Therefore it is necessary that His Holiness no longer
keep the door bolted, but open the depth of his charity to
so many souls who want to serve God truly and whose prayers
for the salvation of His Holiness and the Holy See will
efficaciously come before God. By this His Holiness will
bestow a great benefit on the world, while at the same time

rectifying all the matters discussed above, and will give
the people hope of having good preachers and confessors,
who by their lives and teachings can lift up the church of
God. Let not His Holiness be stopped by false and deceptive
suggestions of tyrannical, wicked, and false friars. Rather,
let him follow the right footsteps of his holy predecessors.
Inspired by God, whenever they saw the observances of monastic rules fallen into ruin and abuse, they always embraced
the only right way of reform: they took refuge with and
clasped to themselves the few who were fervent in wishing
to lead a good life and who were able to do it.[35] Then,
by the shining light of their examples they drew the others
toward the proper observance [of the rules] and away from
[deformed] monastic orders. Remind His Holiness of what
Pope Eugenius [IV] of blessed memory did for your own order
and what was done in our time in Spain, in the province of
the Angels, in Portugal, and elsewhere.[36] More recently,
about seven years ago, obvious necessity constrained your
general chapter to make provisions for the assigning of
some particular places in each province, where, as in places
of refuge, the poor, decent friars could withdraw to observe
their rule. They openly declared in defiance of the scoundrels that it was not possible to follow monastic rules while
remaining with the deformed multitude. But because these
regulations were made on too weak a basis and did not have
their source in the authority of His Holiness and the Holy
See, but only in that of the superior [of the order] and
the general chapter, therefore the result has been first of
all that many good, poor friars who would have been suitable
to such a reformed monastery either were not admitted there
or were recalled and employed elsewhere. Indeed, to the
detriment of the above-mentioned reform, some friars who
were entirely unsuited were sent on purpose to the
good ones, who then were forced to keep them [as part of
their monastic community] because the scoundrels wanted to
be able to say that which they used to say about everyone
who lived a good life, namely that he who serves God

is vain,[37] or insane, or melancholy, and so forth.

In order to convince His Holiness that all this is true, show him the regulation promulgated by the superior [of your order]. Thus [the good friars] have been everywhere persecuted and abandoned; before they are brought entirely low through all these persecutions, may His Holiness deign to hear about the few places belonging to this group, and the purity, Christian simplicity, honor of God, and edification of neighbor in the lives [of the good friars]. His Holiness should consider making arrangements enabling these monasteries to remain safe and not be ruined, since they are constantly threatened by evil friars. Although the needs of the church and the world demand the generosity of His Holiness in granting the gift of a holy and longed-for reform, not only to all true monastic orders, but other [congregations] as well, since all are in need of it, still you should [particularly] plead for your own [Franciscan order], which certainly is in the most dire straits on account of the large number of its members, as has already been stated, and because in the most noble organization the worst corruption now exists. So that your requests may be granted more easily, restrict yourself to your province and your city, if only His Holiness begins to give you a sign of hope, and start from this city [Venice] where [monastic reform] is so desired. Tell His Holiness about the wishes of important people here: give him the petition and show him the regulations of the Father Superior concerning these matters, so that His Holiness can see how little is asked of him, so that [information] about things already done is sent to him, and so that with this easy beginning in such an important province an opportunity is given to him to follow readily in others that are not so important. May His Holiness not leave to others so much merit before God and so much glory! The proposed reform must be brought about in any case, and extreme necessity urges it in such a way that we can no longer stand still. Already His Holiness can see the agitation in the Capuchin order[38] and in others in different

parts of the world: all shout, all are in an uproar and
remain [in their orders] to the extent to which they have
not lost hope in reform. But in the very hour when they
lose such hope, I foresee with certainty that many in
desperation will take reform into their own hands, which
God in his mercy may not allow because we already have so
many tribulations that they fully suffice.

Therefore His Holiness should not hesitate to do this
holy work, which is necessary for monastic orders, useful
for the clergy, beneficial for the people, in accordance
with the practices of the church, opportune against present
calamities, and efficacious against those to come: the Lord
will grant their wish to those who fear him,[39] and the vio-
lent take the Kingdom of Heaven by force.[40] My Father, I
pray to the Majesty of God to grant you his grace so that
when you come before His Holiness, the Reverend Protector
[of your order][41] and the other Reverend fathers, you will
be able to move their hearts to mercy by your effective arguments and piteous tears accompanied by the sighs and
groans of so many good souls.

Since I was forced to speak about grievous matters, I
hope to be able to conclude with something agreeable. I
remember that the Holy Apostolic See used to provide help
to the Christian commonwealth in various kinds of distress
by founding military orders, whose members fought in defense
of the Catholic faith, the holy church, and [performed]
various good works. Thus in Jerusalem the two orders of St.
John and St. Mary of Jerusalem[42] were established for the
defense of the Holy Land against infidels and for the reception of pilgrims visiting the holy places. So also in
various parts of Spain other military orders were established
against the Moors.[43] Thus by the hand of St. Dominic the
army was founded whose members called themselves soldiers of
Christ.[44] Although different in their condition, in the
beginning all were fervent to observe their vows and serve
God and his holy church. As long as the observance of their
vows lasted, the grace of God was with them, and one held

off a thousand, while ten thousand were put to flight by
two.[45] They went forward every day, and God gave them
victory against their enemies; he struck terror in the heart
of their enemies, who dared not resist them. But because
their greatness and riches led to luxury, ostentation, and
licentiousness, they abandoned the observance of their vows
and lost their military discipline. It seems that God has
allowed them then to be humbled and overcome by their
enemies. Thus we have lost beautiful Rhodes,[46] and on the
other side of Europe just recently we have seen that monster,
the general of the above-mentioned order of St. Mary become a
Lutheran.[47] Today we see that our needs and calamities are
not less than those of the past; if the Divine Goodness sent
some kind of help by means of His Holiness, undoubtedly it
would result in great benefits.

Because Divine Providence does not fail when necessary,
His Holiness should be told how the Holy Spirit inspired the
virtuous and generous mind of a certain gentleman[48] in a
certain city, who belongs to a certain military order, the
habit of which he has been wearing for twenty years now.
While in that order, he was made by the Apostolic See a
prelate over two churches, one in the city mentioned, and
the second in a certain other city. He considered that his
rule and profession obliged him to keep the three monastic
vows, and he found himself in a state where he could not
easily do it, because in his order no appearance of monasticism remained any longer, but starting with the dress, all
are mere secular clerics. He wished to keep what he promised
to God so many years ago, and furthermore, inspired by God,
to offer his own abilities, his life and person to the needs
of Holy Church. He wanted to draw to this beautiful enterprise other kind, noble, and good spirits, who also wish to
serve Christ in this way rather than in any other religious
order. He begs His Holiness in his usual providence and
kindness as well as that of the Holy See to grant him the

permission to reform his two churches and to return with
them to the observance of the three essential vows, namely
poverty, chastity, and obedience. [He also asks] to be
allowed to receive all who are inspired by God and who seem
to be suitable for a military order to join him. They
intend to be gathered and instituted principally for the defense of the Catholic faith against heretics and all other
infidels and to devote themselves to hospitality and other
good works. They ask to be subject directly to the Holy
Apostolic See, under the protection of which they wish to
place their churches, and goods, and persons prepared to
live under the rule which shall be given to them by the
said Holy See. Meanwhile they are living in a community,
sharing equally the income from the above-mentioned churches
as well as any pay or alms given them. By papal authority
the two churches should be forever joined with their congregation, and a member of a monastic order or some prelate or
ecclesiastical dignitary should be empowered by apostolic
authority to receive immediately the profession of the
petitioner. By the same papal authority this deputy should
have full power and authority to make provisions and deci-
sions about the color and shape of the habit and pectoral
cross, as well as about the number of "Our Fathers" [to be
prayed daily], other offices, and all the rest of their
regulations, fasts, and appropriate observances. After this
the said petitioner should be able to receive other brethren
who want to make their profession after one probationary
year has elapsed; and from then on his successors in that
office [should have the same authority]. So that affairs
do not become disorderly on account of life-long exercise
of authority by one person, the said petitioner, his companions and successors should be able to hold their chapter
meetings and accept the voluntary resignations of the said
petitioner. Then, through regulations accepted at the chapter meeting, they should be able to make provisions for each
house to have its own prior. Above all, there should be a
master, who could be one of the priors, maybe he who becomes

prior in the most important city. The priors could hold
office for one or three or more years, or whatever seems
best to His Holiness. The petitioner whom I mentioned
might be elected by the chapter first before others since
he is a suitable person, most useful to the whole enterprise.
You, Reverend Father, make His Holiness understand that I
hope this will be something of the greatest service to God
and the pope and of vast importance to other states. Because of this it has seemed well to me to keep it secret;
I hope that this military order will be a fortified tower
of the Catholic faith and of His Holiness. Other gentle
spirits, attracted by the virtue of the petitioner and wishing to serve Christ, as has already been said, long to see
the day which will be happy for all everywhere. Take the
petition and request that His Holiness acknowledge it for
now, because soon an appropriate person will be sent to him
with ample instructions to solicit its expedition. Humbly
beg His Holiness to deign to believe me that in this affair
many matters of importance for the honor of God and His
Holiness are concerned, and I would go on recounting many
and beautiful ones, if I did not fear to be tiresome. But,
God willing, they shall be told, or rather, seen at the
appropriate time, if His Holiness wishes. You, my Father,
faithfully report these few observations [offered in the
spirit] of charity and fidelity and again ask for the blessing of His Holiness, humbly kissing his holy feet.

*6. Proposal of a Select Committee of Cardinals
and other Prelates Concerning the
Reform of the Church, Written and Presented by
Order of His Holiness Pope Paul III (1537)*

A. Introduction

In 1536 Pope Paul III summoned a general council with
the bull *Ad Dominici gregis curam*. It was to meet in
Mantua the following year. Unlike Clement VII, his inde-
cisive predecessor, Paul III realized that delaying the
council further would harm the papacy and increase uncertainty and confusion among the faithful. After Luther had
become a public figure in 1517, appeals for a council were
made by both his adherents and opponents. But such diverse
factors as the death of Pope Adrian VI in 1523, the timid
personality of Pope Clement VII, the Habsburg-Valois wars,
the opposition of Lutherans to a meeting outside Germany,
and the tension between proponents and opponents of a
council among papal advisers were serious obstacles to its
convocation. Not until 1545 did the first session of the
council open at Trent--too late to change the fact of a
split in Western Christianity.

As a preliminary step to the planned meeting at Mantua,
the Pope called together nine prelates to begin the prepara-
tory work and make recommendations for dealing with the most
pressing problems of the church. The group included some
of the most outspoken Catholic advocates of reform. The
Pope had asked Cardinal Contarini for his help in choosing
outstanding men who could initiate reform in Rome, and the
latter did not hesitate to bring to the Pope's attention
those of his friends who most shared his desire for change
in the church. Besides Reginald Pole, the cousin of King
Henry VIII of England, and the only non-Italian in the
group, they were Gianpietro Carafa (the later Pope Paul IV),
bishops Jacopo Sadoleto, Federico Fregoso, and Gian Matteo

Giberti, the Benedictine abbot Gregorio Cortese, the
Dominican theologian Tommaso Badia, and Jerome Aleander,
best known as a papal diplomat.

Toward the end of November, 1536, the commission met in
Rome. The opening address was made by Sadoleto, who sharply attacked corruption in the church, blaming the papacy
and curia. No information about the discussion of the
commission during the next few months has come to light;
its members had taken an oath of secrecy, and they observed
it.

On March 9, 1537, the written memorial which follows
was presented to the Pope in a consistory. Copies were
distributed to cardinals who wished to discuss it with
their advisers. The text soon found its way to printers in
Rome. In 1538 the document appeared in a German translation,
and Luther edited it with a preface and extremely caustic
marginal comments. Unwilling to admit the sincerity of the
prelates who wrote it, Luther considered them hypocrites
bent on supporting the papacy in misleading Christianity
further.

The college of cardinals was sharply divided about the
report. A conservative, inert majority was not interested
in change. Contarini and his associates were too small a
group to put their ideas into practice unaided. An
equally small group of intelligent and articulate curialists
was their main opponent, fighting with much support for that
which most cardinals and curial officials wanted: no radical
change.

The immediate significance of the report should not be
overstated. On the basis of the text alone it would be
easy to point to the memorial as the beginning of a new
approach to questions of reform in Rome. However, the real
issues were whether it would become the inspiration of
decrees and laws and whether these laws would be strictly
enforced. Everything depended on papal support, and Paul
III was not a zealous or impatient reformer. He consulted

all the cardinals and was guided by the unfavorable and
critical opinions of the majority in his decision not to
put the recommendations into practice at that time.

In spite of its failure to gain acceptance at the
papal court, the report is a significant document in
Italian reform thought. Interest in it persisted, as
shown by thirteen printings and three translations in the
two decades after its appearance. The first question it
raised remained a fundamental one for subsequent thinkers
about church reform. It concerned the nature of papal
power. The authors of the proposal saw all abuses in
the church as stemming from the same source: exaggerated
claims made by curial jurists about the absolute character
of papal power, and their belief that the pope could do
what he pleased with both material and spiritual goods
of the church.

Rome was held responsible not only for abuses, but also
for the lack of discipline and order within the hierarchy.
The proposal could hardly have been more outspoken in its
criticism of existing conditions in the Catholic church.
It stressed that the pope and bishops must become models of
Christian pastors, truly serving their flock; only then
could order be established in the dioceses and parishes.

The most conspicuous defect of the proposal was its
failure to mention ways of dealing with doctrinal reform
and with the complex question of the relation between central, intermediate, and local authority in the church.
Despite the profoundly serious challenge of the Protestant
Reformation to both doctrine and structure of the Roman
church, the proposal is striking in its expression of an
old-fashioned view of reform, which could be summarized
by quoting the adage *"purga Romam, purgatur mundus!"*--pur-
ify Rome and the world will be cleansed. Nowhere are
basic structural or doctrinal changes contemplated.

The authors of the proposal certainly made numerous
compromises before presenting the final version to Pope
Paul III. Whatever their individual views of reform, they

endorsed what Carafa had already stressed in his memorial
of 1532: that change should proceed in an institutional
framework, and that its objective was the upholding, purifying, and revitalizing of a basically acceptable ecclesiastical order.

For a discussion of the proposal see Hubert Jedin,
History of the Council of Trent, Vol. I (St. Louis: Herder,
1957), pp. 423-33. The entire volume is devoted to the
background of the council and presents a complex view of the
difficulties preceding its first meeting. See also Richard
Douglas, *Jacopo Sadoleto* (Cambridge, Mass.: Harvard University Press, 1959), pp. 109-114. Luther's translation and
comments are available in English in *Luther's Works*. American Edition, Vol. 34: Career of the Reformer (Philadelphia:
Muhlenberg Press, 1960), pp. 231-267.

The text is translated from: "Consilium delectorum
cardinalium et aliorum praelatorum de emendanda ecclesia
S.D.N. Paulo III iubente conscriptum et exhibitum," in
*Concilium Tridentinum. Diariorum Actorum Epistularum
Tractatuum nova collectio*. Ed. Societas Goerresiana, Vol.
XII (Freiburg im Breisgau: Herder, 1929), pp. 131-145.

B. Text

I.

Most holy Father! We are so unable to express in words
how grateful Christendom should be to almighty God because
he has appointed you pope and shepherd of his flock at this
time and caused you to entertain your present purpose,
that we have no hope of conceiving in what fashion due and
proper thanks should be given to God. For the Spirit of
God, by whom the powers of heaven were made firm, as the
prophet says,[1] has decided to restore through you the
church of Christ, which is tottering, and, in truth, about
to collapse headlong into ruin, to support her ruinous
fabric by your hand (as we already see done), to lift
her to her former eminence and bring her back to her
pristine beauty. We, whom Your Holiness summoned, are
going to present what we take to be a most certain conjecture of this divine plan. You ordered that without any
regard either to your own interest or that of anyone else
we should point out to you the abuses, indeed the most
serious ills with which the church of God and especially
the court of Rome have long been afflicted. As these
pernicious diseases have grown steadily though insensibly
graver, they have brought the church to that ruinous
condition in which we now see her.

Your Holiness, instructed by the Spirit of God, who (as
Augustine says) speaks in our hearts without the sound of
words,[2] knows well that the beginning of these ills goes
back to the fact that some popes, your predecessors, having
itching ears, as the apostle Paul says,[3] provided themselves
with teachers according to their own desire, not to learn
from them what they should do, but that through the zeal and
cunning of these men a reason might be found by which that

which pleased them might be made lawful. Moreover, flat-
tery follows every eminent person as the shadow does the
body, and it has always been most difficult for truth to
gain access to the ears of princes. Hence it has happened
that immediately teachers appeared, who taught that the
pope was lord of all benefices.[4] Thus, since a lord legally
can sell what is his own, it necessarily follows that the
pope cannot be guilty of simony,[5] because the will of the
pope, whatever it may be, is the rule governing his deci-
sions and actions. From this follows without a doubt that
he may lawfully do whatever he pleases.

From this source, just as from the Trojan horse,
very many abuses and grave ills have invaded the church of
God. Because of them we now see her suffering and almost
despairing of ever being delivered and cured. The report
of these things has spread to the infidels (let Your Holiness believe us who know!), who mock the Christian faith
especially for this reason, so that through us--and we
stress through us--the name of Christ is blasphemed among
the nations.

But you, most Holy Father (which you truly are), besides
being renowned for your prudence, now also instructed by the
Spirit of God, when you devoted yourself entirely to the
charge of seeing that the church of Christ given to your
care may be healed of her diseases and recover her health,
have correctly seen that the cure must begin where the
disease took its origin. Following the teaching of the
apostle Paul you want to be not a master but a steward,[6]
to be found faithful by the Lord, taking as an example
that servant whom in the Gospel the Lord set over his household to give them food in due season.[7] For this reason you
have resolved to desire nothing unlawful, nor wish to have
the power of doing what you ought not. Therefore you have
summoned us; although inexperienced and unequal to so great

a task, we are deeply concerned with the honor and glory
of Your Holiness and especially with the renewal of the
church of Christ. With the gravest words you ordered us
to draw up a list of all abuses and to make them known to
you, adjuring us earnestly that we will have to answer to
God if we fulfill the task required of us negligently and
unfaithfully. So that we might treat everything more
freely among ourselves and then explain it to you, you have
bound us by oath under penalty of excommunication not to
reveal to anyone what has been entrusted to us.

Obeying your command, we have therefore listed as briefly as possible the diseases and such remedies as we could
suggest in spite of our limited abilities. You, however,
in your goodness and wisdom will correct and perfect all
that is unsatisfactory because of our lack of competence.
In order to keep our work within certain limits, however,
since Your Holiness is ruler of territories belonging to the
church, pope of the universal church, and also bishop of
Rome, we will say nothing about matters pertaining to the
states of the church, which we see excellently governed by
your wisdom. We shall deal with questions pertaining to the
office of the universal pontiff, and some which concern
the bishop of Rome.

In our opinion one thing should be stated before all
others, most Holy Father, which Aristotle says in his
Politics: as in any commonwealth, so also in the government
of the church of Christ, the principal law should be that
as far as possible all other laws be observed.[8] Let us not
think ourselves empowered to grant dispensations from them,
unless there exists an urgent and necessary reason. No more
pernicious custom can be introduced into any commonwealth
than the failure to observe the laws, which our ancestors
wanted to be sacred, and whose authority they called venerable and divine. You know all these things, Holy Father,
having read them before in the writings of philosophers and

theologians. There is also another matter which we consider
not of equal but of very much greater importance: it should
not be lawful, even for the Vicar of Christ, to obtain any
wealth through the use of the power of the keys given him
by Christ. For this is Christ's command: "Freely you have
received, freely you shall give."[9]

II.

After having established these points first, let Your
Holiness then take care of the church of Christ in such a
way as to have many ministers through whom you may fulfill
that charge. These ministers are all the clergy, to whom
the divine service is entrusted, especially the priests,
most particularly the parish priests, and above all the
bishops. Thus, if your government is to function properly,
the first task is to make sure that these ministers are fit
for the offices which they are to perform.

[1] The first abuse is the ordination of clerics,
especially priests, in which neither care nor diligence is
employed. Everywhere those that are least educated, of
lowest birth, conspicuous for their bad habits, or too young
are admitted to holy orders and especially to the priesthood,
the sign which above all others makes Christ manifest. From
this cause stem countless scandals and contempt of the
clergy; for this reason respect for divine worship is
not only diminished, but well-nigh extinct. We think that
it would be best if Your Holiness first entrusted in Rome two
or three prelates, who are learned and upright men, with the
task of supervising the ordination of clerics. Then you
might order all bishops, even under penalty of censure, to
do likewise in their dioceses. Your holiness should not
permit anyone to be ordained except by his bishop or with
his permission, or that of the prelates appointed for this
purpose in Rome. Moreover, each bishop should appoint in his
church a master by whom young clerics in minor orders are to
be instructed in learning and proper conduct, as the law
requires.[10]

[2]   Another extremely grave abuse consists in be-
stowing ecclesiastical benefices, especially parishes, and
above all bishoprics. Here the custom has come to prevail
of providing for persons on whom the benefices are conferred, not for the flock of Christ and the church. Therefore in granting the benefices of parishes, and especially
bishoprics, care must be taken that they be conferred on
good and learned men, who can themselves discharge the
duties attached to the benefices, and above all on those
who are likely to remain in residence. Thus a benefice in
Spain or Britain should not be conferred on an Italian, or
vice versa. This rule should be observed in regard to ap-
pointments, to benefices that become vacant through death,
as well as resignations, where now such great consideration
is given to the wishes of him who resigns and to nothing
else. We would consider it a good idea if one or more
honest men were appointed to supervise this matter of
resignations.

[3]   Another abuse has crept in when benefices are conferred or ceded to others: pensions are set up from their
revenues. Indeed, sometimes he who resigns a benefice
reserves all its income for himself. In this matter it
should be noted that pensions cannot be set up and justified
for any other reason than to provide alms which should be
given for pious uses and to the poor. For the revenues are
attached to the benefice as the body to the soul. By their
nature they belong to him who holds the benefice, to enable
him to live on them honestly as befits his rank, and at the
same time to sustain the expenses of divine worship and the
repair of the church and its appurtenant buildings. What
is left he should spend for pious purposes. Such, then,
is the nature of these revenues. But just as in nature
some things occur by a particular movement of nature which
lies outside her ordinary course and inclination, so if the
pope, the universal steward of church property, sees that

all or part of the portion of revenues which should be
used for pious purposes could be better employed for some
godly use other than the actual one, he can doubtless provide accordingly. Therefore he may lawfully impose a tax
on benefices for the support of an indigent person, especially a cleric, so that the latter can lead an honest life
befitting his rank. Thus it is a great abuse to reserve
the whole revenue of a benefice and to take away all that
should be allotted for divine service and the support of
its holder. Likewise, it is certainly a great abuse to
give pensions to rich clerics who can live comfortably and
honorably on the incomes they already have. Both of these
abuses should be done away with.

[4] Still another abuse consists in the exchange of
benefices, done by agreements which are all simoniacal,
and where no regard is shown for anything but profit.

[5] Another abuse which must be completely eradicated
has prevailed at this court thanks to the cunning of some
shrewd and skillful men. Since it is stipulated by law
that benefices cannot be bequeathed by last will and testament, because they do not belong to the testator but to
the church, and that possessions of the church should be
preserved for the common good of all faithful rather than
becoming the private estate of some individual, therefore
human (but not Christian) ingenuity has invented many ways
by which to make a mockery of this law. First, bishoprics
and other benefices are resigned on condition that the old
occupant may resume them again. To this is added the
reservation of income to him who resigns, as well as the
collation[11] of benefices; this is topped off by the reten-
tion of his right to administer the diocese. By such an
agreement a bishop is created who has none of the rights
and powers of a bishop, while to the other, who is not a
bishop at all, belong all the prerogatives of one. May
Your Holiness realize the results of the teaching of
flatterers, by which it has come to pass that all that
pleases is permitted! What else is this than appointing an

heir to one's benefice? Still another fraud has been
invented: to bishops who request it coadjutors are given,
less well qualified than they. Thus, unless a man deliberately wants to shut his eyes, he must clearly see that
coadjutors become heirs in this way.

[6] Moreover, there exists an old law restored by
Pope Clement,[12] to the effect that sons of priests cannot
possess the benefices of their fathers, so that common
goods of the church should not become private property by
this means. This venerable law is being dispensed with,
as we hear. We do not wish to conceal a fact which every
intelligent person recognizes as the unadorned truth:
nothing has inflamed the hatred for clerics (which has
caused so much dissension already, while still more is
threatening) more than the turning of goods and revenues
of the church from common into private property. Before,
all men had hope that these abuses would be corrected;
now they are reduced to despair and speak evil against
the Holy See.

[7] Another abuse consists in the matter of expectation[13] and reservation[14] of benefices. Occasion is given
to one man to desire the death of another and to be glad
when he hears of it. Thus when benefices fall vacant, abler
and more worthy men are barred from having access to them.
These practices also cause litigation. We think that all
these abuses must be corrected.

[8] Another abuse was invented by the same cunning.
By law certain benefices are incompatible, and are so
called.[15] Through the significance of the term *beneficia
incompatibilia* our ancestors wished to admonish us that
they must not be conferred on one person. But now dispensations are granted to hold not only two but more
benefices, and even bishoprics, which is worse. We maintain
that this custom, which has become so prevalent because of
avarice, must be abolished, especially when bishoprics are
concerned. What shall we say about the union [or amalga-
mation] of benefices for the duration of a man's lifetime,

so that plurality of benefices should not stand in the way
of his possessing incompatible ones?   Is this not mere
circumvention of the law?

[9]   Another abuse has prevailed: to the cardinals are
granted or given *in commendam*[16] not just one but many
bishoprics.   Holy Father, we consider this practice to be
of grave consequence for the church of God, first of all
because the offices of a cardinal and a bishop are incompatible in the same person.   The function of cardinals is to
assist Your Holiness in governing the universal church; that
of the bishop, to tend his flock.   He cannot do this properly and as he ought unless he lives with his sheep, as the
shepherd with his flock.[17]

Besides, Holy Father, this practice does great harm by
the example it sets.   How could the Holy See straighten out
and correct the abuses of others if it tolerates abuses
among its most eminent members?   We do not think that they
should be allowed to break the law more easily because they
are cardinals; on the contrary!   Their lives should be a
model for others, for one should not imitate the Pharisees
who speak and do not act, but our Saviour Jesus Christ who
began to act and then to teach.   This custom does great
harm in the deliberations of church affairs, for such an
abuse foments avarice.   Because of it cardinals solicit
bishoprics from kings and princes, on whom they then become
dependent.   They cannot freely express their opinion; indeed,
even if they could and wanted to, they would deceive themselves, since their judgment is warped by affection and
interest.   If only this practice would be abolished and
all cardinals be given an equal income which would enable
them to live honestly according to their rank!   We are of
the opinion that this could easily be done, if we would
be willing to serve no longer mammon, but Christ alone.[18]

III.

[1]   After censuring abuses that concern the appointment
of your ministers, who are like instruments through whom
the worship of God should be properly conducted, and the
Christian people well instructed and governed, we proceed
to matters which pertain to the government of this same
people. Here, most Holy Father, we find an abuse which must
be corrected first, before all others. First and foremost
the bishops, but then the parish priests as well, must not
be absent from their churches and parishes, unless for some
weighty reason. They must be in residence, especially the
bishops, as we already have said, since they are the husbands
of the church committed to their care. By our immortal
God, what more miserable sight could present itself to a
Christian travelling through Christendom than the deserted
state of the churches? Almost all shepherds have abandoned
their flocks, nearly all of which are entrusted to hirelings.
Therefore a severe penalty and no mere censure should be
imposed especially on bishops, but also on parish priests
who are absent form their flocks. Let the absentees
receive no income, unless bishops ask for your permission
and parish priests for that of their bishops for a short
absence. In this regard regulations and conciliar
decrees should be read, which provide that a bishop shall
not be absent from his church longer than three Sundays.[19]

[2]   It also constitutes an abuse that so many of the
most reverend cardinals are absent from the court of Rome
and perform only a part of the duties attached to their
office. Perhaps not all should be here, for we consider
it useful that some should live in their own countries;
through them, as through roots spread throughout all of
Christendom, the peoples are kept in obedience to the
Roman See. Yet Your Holiness should summon most of them
to your court, where they should reside. In this way the
cardinals, besides discharging their duties, would enhance
the grandeur of your court. They would also fill the gap

left there by the departure of many bishops, who would
have returned to their churches.

[3] Another great and insufferable abuse, by which the
entire Christian people are scandalised, arises from impedi-
ments imposed upon bishops in the government of their flock,
and especially in the punishment and correction of evildoers. In the first place, evil men, above all clerics,
exempt themselves through many ways from the jurisdiction
of their bishop. Next, if they are not exempt, they
immediately have recourse to the Penitentiary or the
Datary, where they speedily find a way of escaping punishment, and what is worse, upon payment of money. This
scandal, most Holy Father, creates such disorder among the
Christian people that we cannot express it in words. We
beseech Your Holiness by the blood of Christ, through which
he redeemed his church, washing her with this same blood:
do away with these stains. If these evils were to gain a
foothold in any earthly republic or kingdom, it would
immediately or very shortly afterward fall headlong into
ruin, and nothing could prolong its existence. Yet we
think that we can with impunity introduce these abominations into Christendom![20]

[4] Another abuse to be corrected concerns monastic
orders. So many of them are in such a deplorable condition
that they are a scandal and a pernicious example to the
secular clergy. In our opinion all conventual[21] orders
should be abolished, not through unjust harshness toward
anyone but by prohibiting them to admit novices. In this
way they would be quickly destroyed without wronging anyone,
and good religious could be appointed in their stead. We
think it would be best if all boys who are not professed
were removed from their monasteries.

[5] We think that the following should be observed and
set straight when friars are appointed as preachers and
confessors: their superiors should first apply themselves
with great diligence to determining that they are qualified.
Then they should be presented to the bishops, to whom before

all others the care of the church is entrusted, and examined
by them or by men suitable for this task. Without their
consent the friars should not be allowed to carry on these
activities.[22]

[6] We have already said, most Holy Father, that it is
unlawful in any way to obtain gain through the use of the
keys. Here the words of Christ are immutable: "Freely you
have received, freely you shall give." This does not only
pertain to Your Holiness, but to all who share in your
power; thus we would wish your legates and nuncios to give
heed to it as well. For as the usage which now prevails
brings dishonor to the Holy See and confusion to the people,
so, if the contrary were to happen, it would redound greatly
to the glory of the former and lead to the wonderful edification of the latter.

[7] Another abuse distresses the Christian people
through the nuns who are under the care of conventual friars.
In a great many monasteries public sacrilege is committed to
the greatest scandal of all men. Let Your Holiness take
the care of nuns from conventual friars and give it either
to ordinaries[23] or others, as it seems best to you.

[8] A great and pernicious abuse exists in universities,
especially in Italy where many professors of philosophy
teach impiety. Indeed, in the churches utterly godless
disputations take place, and even in the seemingly pious
ones sacred topics are treated in a most irreverent fashion
before the people. We therefore think that wherever there
are public schools, the bishops should be required to admonish instructors not to teach impiety to young men. Rather,
they should guide them to piety, pointing out to them the
weakness of natural understanding in questions pertaining
to God, to the recent origin or eternity of the world, and
the like. Similarly, bishops should not permit public disputations of such questions or of theological topics, which
thus only lose the respect of the common people. These
matters should be disputed privately, and other questions of
natural philosophy in public.

All bishops, especially of larger cities, where
such disputations customarily take place, should be required
to comply with these regulations.

The same care should be employed in the printing of
books by writing to all princes to be on their guard lest
all sorts of books be printed throughout their territories.
This matter should be entrusted to the care of the ordinaries. [24]

Because it is common nowadays to read to grammar school
boys the *Colloquies* of Erasmus, which contain many things
inciting uneducated minds to impiety, it should be forbidden
to read them as well as other books of their kind in the
schools. [25]

IV.

Having treated matters pertaining to the appointment of
your ministers for pastoral work and administration of the
universal church, we would like to call the attention of
Your Holiness to the question of dispensations granted by
you. In addition to the abuses mentioned above still
further ones have been introduced.

[1] The first concerns apostate friars and monks, who
leave their orders after having taken solemn vows and obtain
dispensations from wearing the habit of their order or even
a trace of it, but instead don fine clerical dress. Let
us not speak at this point of the profit involved. We have
already said in the beginning that it is unlawful to amass
wealth through the use of the keys and the power received
from Christ, and we hold that dispensations must no longer
be granted in such cases. For the habit is the sign of
one's calling, to which these apostates should be held, and
from which not even the bishop can dispense them. Such a
dispensation should not be granted to them; neither should
they be permitted to have benefices or ministries, since
they have broken their vow by which they pledged themselves
to God. [26]

[2]   Another abuse lies in the existence of collectors
of the Holy Spirit, of St. Anthony, and the like, who
deceive country people and simple souls, entangling them
in countless superstitions. We believe that these collectors should be done away with.[27]

[3]   Still another abuse is the granting of dispensations to marry to those who have taken holy orders. No
such dispensation should be given to anyone unless is it
for the purpose of preserving some people or nation, where
there exists a serious reason of public concern. This
should be especially observed now, when the Lutherans
force the issue.

[4]   It is an abuse to grant dispensations for marriages
between close relatives and kindred. We think that this
definitely should not be done for persons related in the
second degree, unless for some weighty public reason.
More distant relations should be dispensed only for good
reasons, and without a fine, as we already have said. The
only exception would be if they were already married. Then
it would be lawful to impose a monetary penalty for absolution from sins already committed and to destine the money
to pious purposes that Your Holiness supports. For just as
no money can be demanded when the keys are used properly
and without incurring sin by the pope, so he can impose a
fine and destine it for pious purposes in cases where
absolution from sins is asked.

[5]   Another abuse is the absolution of those guilty of
simony. Alas, to such an extent does this destructive vice
prevail in the church of God, that some are not ashamed to
commit simony and then quickly ask for absolution from
punishment. They buy the absolution, and in this way retain
the benefice which they bought before. We are not saying
that Your Holiness cannot remit them the punishment which
is laid down by positive law. But we are of the opinion
that Your Holiness should not do it under any circumstances,
so that this terrible evil, than which nothing is more
pernicious or scandalous, might be stopped.

[6]   Clergymen should not be permitted to dispose of
church property through their wills, unless in very excep-
tional cases, so that the goods belonging by right to the
poor might not be used for private pleasure and ever more
building.

[7]   The right of hearing confessions with the use of
a portable altar should not be granted lightly. For in
this way both ecclesiastical functions and the most excellent sacrament are made commonplace.[28]

[8]   Indulgences should not be granted more than once
a year in each large city.

[9]   Neither commutation of vows nor substitution for
them should be readily allowed, unless it be for some
equivalent good.

[10]   It has been customary to change the last will of
testators who have bequeathed a certain amount of money for
charitable purposes. By the authority of Your Holiness
this money is transferred to the heir or legatees under the
pretext of their poverty, but in reality for a money payment. Unless a great change occurs in the family of the
heir through the death of the testator, who probably would
have changed his will had he foreseen it, it is wrong to
alter his wishes. Concerning money, we have said often
enough why we think the church should hold herself altogether aloof from it.

V.

[1]   Having laid before you as clearly as we could all
those matters which concern the pontiff of the universal
church, we should say some things pertaining to the bishop
of Rome. The city and church of Rome is the mother and
teacher of other churches; thus, divine worship and virtuous
customs should be especially conspicuous here. For this
reason, most Holy Father, all strangers are scandalised who
enter St. Peter's basilica, where slovenly and ignorant
priests celebrate mass, dressed in vestments and attire

with which they could not really appear even in a squalid
house. This is a great offense to all. Therefore the
reverend archpriest or the penitentiary should be charged
with removing this scandal. In other churches the same
should be done.

[2] In this city courtesans go about or ride on mules
like honest women. In broad daylight they are followed
by men of noble families who are members of households of
cardinals, and by clerics. In no other city do we see such
corruption save in this, which should be an example to all
others. Moreover, these women live in fine houses. This
shameful abuse must be corrected.

[3] Hate and enmity between private citizens exist in
this city. It is a particular concern of the bishop to
unite and reconcile them. Therefore some cardinals most
suitable for this task, especially native Romans, should
be appointed to settle all quarrels and reconcile the
citizens with each other.

[4] In Rome there are hospitals, orphans, and widows.
Their care belongs above all to their bishop and sovereign.
Your Holiness could duly take care of them through some
upright and honest cardinals.

These, then, Holy Father, are the points which we have
drawn up at present as far as we are able, and which in our
opinion must be changed. But you in your goodness and
wisdom will judge everything better. If we did not do
justice to these matters, which are much greater than our
ability to deal with them, at least we have satisfied our
consciences. We have the greatest hope that during your
reign we shall see the church of God purified, beautiful as
a dove, at peace and in harmony with herself, united in
one body, remembering your name forever. You have assumed
the name of Paul; we hope you will imitate his charity. He
was the chosen vessel to make known the name of Christ among
the gentiles. Our hope is that you are truly chosen to
restore to our hearts and actions the name of Christ, which
is forgotten by the nations and by us, the clergy, to heal

our diseases, to lead the sheep of Christ to one fold, and
to turn away from us the wrath of God and the vengeance
we deserve, which is hanging over our heads and ready to
fall on us.

Cardinal Gasparo Contarini[29]
Cardinal Gianpietro Carafa[30]
Cardinal Giacopo Sadoleto[31]
Cardinal Reginald Pole[32]
Federico Fregoso, archbishop of Salerno[33]
Girolamo Aleandro, archbishop of Brindisi[34]
Gian Matteo Giberti, bishop of Verona[35]
Gregorio Cortese, abbot of San Giorgio in Venice[36]
Tommaso Badia, master of the sacred palace[37]

III. The Break with Institutions and Doctrines

7. THE *BENEFICIO DI CRISTO*

A. Introduction

The *Beneficio di Cristo* is the most famous work associated with the Italian Reformation. It was first printed anonymously in Venice in 1543, where large numbers of copies were sold during the next six years, according to the testimony of a contemporary.[1] The "little book," as it was often called, was received enthusiastically elsewhere as well. For example, at least three cardinals who had been among the signers of the *Consilium de emendanda ecclesia* knew it well. The first, Giovanni Morone, as bishop of Modena not only approved the book but promoted its sale in his diocese.[2] The Benedictine Gregorio Cortese esteemed the work so highly that he declared: "When I dress in the morning, I cannot cloak myself in anything better than this *Beneficio di Cristo*."[3] Tommaso Badia, the papal theologian, also approved the book highly.[4]

In 1549 the *Beneficio* was prohibited by the inquisition and was suppressed so successfully that no Italian copy was found until the mid-nineteenth century, when one belonging to the first edition came to light in the library of St. John's College, Cambridge. Other copies and translations have been found since, and the work has taken its eminent place in Italian Reformation literature.

In spite of continued interest of scholars in the *Beneficio* and a splendid new edition by Salvatore Caponetto,[5] there remain some problems to be solved about the work. The first concerns its authorship. Extant sources indicate that it was written by a Benedictine monk, Benedetto of Mantua, but revised by Marcantonio Flaminio. How much he may have altered the original text is debatable; a recent study carefully advances ingenious and often convincing hypotheses about the extent and nature of Flaminio's contributions.[6]

Other issues still debated include the thorny question
of the work's indebtedness to Luther, Calvin, Melanchthon,
and Valdés.[7] It is possible to find not only echoes but
paraphrases of their writings in the *Beneficio*. But how
to evaluate that fact is another matter. One scholar has
maintained that the *Beneficio* is basically a summary of
passages from the 1539 edition of Calvin's *Institutes*.[8]
Others have argued that approaching the work along these
lines tends to remove it from the center of Italian religious concerns at the time and to endow it with the
character of a mere vehicle for the transmission of ideas
of northern reformers. Thus it would have its sources in
the thought of men foreign to the Italian religious scene.

Some reasons for the appeal of the *Beneficio* were
suggested by the great French historian Lucien Febvre over
forty years ago.[9] Whatever its roots, the work certainly
shows the yearning for a return to biblical Christianity
and insists on the necessity of reforming the individual
on the basis of personal, direct experience. These were
concerns common to men and women throughout Europe, and
they formed a crucial element in sixteenth-century religious
history. The work is unorthodox in the light of Tridentine
doctrinal definitions and belongs to an era before the rigid
separation of Protestant and Catholic spirituality and
theology. It is perhaps the best testimony to the compli-
cated nature of Italian participation in the European
movement for reform of the Christian church and people.

Another reason for the attraction of the *Beneficio*
may have been its style, which is straightforward and
direct, employing non-technical vocabulary. The work could
be read by laymen without much knowledge of theology while
containing ideas sufficiently complex to appeal to the
educated and move them. The central issue of the *Beneficio*
is justification by faith alone. Again and again the main
theme is repeated: the highest good mankind has received
from God is the benefit of Christ's death. Man responds
to God by a loving, trusting, and ultimately justifying

faith. While reliance on works alone is condemned sharply, it is stressed that genuine good works cannot be separated from this faith any more than light can be separated from the flame that is its source. The Pauline image of Christ as the groom appears: Christ's bride, the soul, brings him a dowry of sin, which he accepts and annihilates through his cross.

The work is important as testimony to the intense preoccupation with justification, faith, and works so noticeable in Italian religious thought in the early part of the sixteenth century. In it answers to deeply felt personal religious problems are given in simple and clear fashion. "Reform" for someone immersed in the ideas of the *Beneficio* meant establishing a personal relation with God and had as its condition the turning away from sin, which was an act motivated by love and made in response to grace. If this way of thought were followed to its logical conclusion, questions of dogma, doctrine, and Church organization would at most become peripheral and irrelevant to the central concern of the individual. This the inquisitors understood when they prohibited the book.

The literature dealing with the *Beneficio* is vast. In English, the fullest discussion now is the excellent introduction to: *The Beneficio di Cristo*. Translated, with an Introduction, by Ruth Prelowski, in the *The Proceedings of the Unitarian Historical Society*, XIV, parts I and II (1962-1963) [Italian Reformation Studies in Honor of Laelius Socinus (1562-1962), edited by John A. Tedeschi], pp. 21-102. This translation includes an extensive bibliography. Since then the following important works have appeared, each with full bibliographies: Valdo Vinay, "Die Schrift 'Il Beneficio di Gesù Cristo' und ihre Verbreitung in Europa nach der neueren Forschung," *Archiv für Reformationsgeschichte*, 58 (1967), pp. 29-72. Carlo Ginzburg and Adriano Prosperi, "Le due redazioni del "Beneficio di Cristo," *Eresia e Riforma nell' Italia del Cinquecento*. Miscellanea I [Biblioteca del Corpus Reformatorum Italicorum] (De Kalb, Ill.: Northern Illinois University Press and Chicago: The

Newberry Library, 1974), pp. 135-204, and their *Giochi di
Pazienza. Un Seminario sul "Beneficio di Cristo"* (Turin:
Einaudi, 1975). Tommaso Bozza, *Nuovi studi sulla Riforma
in Italia. I. Il Beneficio di Cristo* (Rome: Edizioni di
Storia e Letteratura, 1976). Paolo Simoncelli, "Nuove
ipotesi e studi sul 'Beneficio di Cristo'," *Critica Storica,*
XII (1975), pp. 321-388.

Dr. Prelowski's translation with slight editorial
changes is reprinted here in its entirety, together with
her references to biblical and patristic citations. The
reader interested in references to the works of Valdés and
the northern reformers should consult both Ruth Prelowski's
and Salvatore Caponetto's annotations.

B. Text

Chapter I
On Original Sin and the Misery of Man

The Holy Scripture says that God created man in his own
image and likeness,[10] making him impassible[11] in regard to
his body and just, truthful, pious, merciful, and holy in
regard to his mind. But when, overcome by greed for knowledge, he ate of the apple forbidden by God, he lost that
divine image and likeness, and became like the animals and
like the devil who had deceived him. In regard to his mind,
he became unjust, lying, cruel, impious, and hostile to God,
and in regard to his body, he became passible[12] and subject
to a thousand inconveniences and infirmities, not only
similar but even inferior to brute animals. If our first
parents had remained obedient to God, they would have left
us their justice and holiness as an inheritance. Instead,
because of their disobedience, they willed us their unrighteousness, impiety, and hatred towards God, so that it is
impossible for us to love God through our own efforts and
to conform to his will. On the contrary, we are hostile
to him, regarding him as a judge who justly punishes our

sins, and we can never rely on his mercy. In short, our
nature has become completely corrupted through the sin of
Adam, and although at first it was superior to all creatures, then it became subject to all of them, a servant of
the devil, of sin, and of death, and condemned to the
miseries of hell. It lost the power of judging things, and
began to call the good evil, and evil good, and to consider
false things as true, and true false. Reflecting on this,
the prophet says that every man is a liar,[13] and that there
is no one who does good,[14] since the devil, like a strongly
armed man, peacefully rules his palace, that is, this world,
of which he became the prince and lord. There is no language that could express a thousandth part of our calamity,
that we who were created by God's own hands, have lost that
divine image and have become like the devil, acquiring his
nature and identity, so that we want everything he does and
equally reject all that displeases him. Because we have so
abandoned ourselves to this evil spirit, each of us is ready
to commit even the gravest sin, unless we are restrained by
the grace of God.

This loss of justice and the inclination and readiness
towards every unrighteousness and impiety is called original
sin, and we carry it with us from the womb of our mother, so
that we are born children of wrath;[15] it originated in our
first parents, and it is the cause and source of all our
vices and the iniquities that we commit. It we wish to be
freed from these things and to return to that first innocence, regaining the image of God, we must first recognize
our misery. For no one ever looks for a doctor unless he
knows he is sick, and he does not acknowledge the excellence
of the doctor or the debt he owes him, unless he recognizes
that his illness is pestilential and deadly. In the same
way, no one recognizes Christ, who is the only doctor for
our souls, unless he sees that his soul is sick. Also he
cannot know Christ's excellence or the obligation that he
has towards him, unless he comes to realize his grievous

sins and his pestilential illness, contracted through the
contagion of our first parents.

Chapter II
That God gave us the Law so that we Would
Recognize our Sin, and Despairing of our Ability
to Justify Ourselves by Works,
Would have Recourse to the Mercy of
God and the Justice of Faith

Accordingly, when our God in his infinite goodness and
mercy wanted to send his only-begotten Son to free the
miserable children of Adam, he knew that first it was
necessary to persuade them of their misery, and so he
elected Abraham, in whose seed he promised to bless all
nations, and accepted his descendants as his special people.[16] After they had left Egypt and were freed from
Pharaoh's bondage, he gave them the Law by means of Moses.
The Law prohibits concupiscence and commands us to love God
with our whole heart, our whole soul, and our whole
strength,[17] so that all our hope is placed in God, and we
are ready to give up our life for our God, to suffer every
bodily torment, to deprive ourselves of our wealth, dignity,
and honours in order to honour God, choosing to die rather
than to do anything, however small, that is not pleasing
to our God, and doing all these things with joy and readiness of heart. Next the Law commands us to love our
neighbor as ourselves,[18] and by neighbor it means every
kind of man, enemies as well as friends;[19] it requires that
we be prepared to do unto everyone what we want done unto
us, and that we care about others' affairs as we would
about our own.

When man looks into this holy Law, as if into a clear
mirror, he soon recognizes his own infirmity and his inca-
pacity to obey God's commandments and to render the honour
and love due to his Creator. Therefore, the first office
performed by the Law is to make sin known, as St. Paul
states,[20] and he says elsewhere: "I did not recognize sin

other than through the Law."[21] The second office performed
by the Law is to make sin grow; for since we have separated
ourselves from obedience to God and have become slaves to
the devil, full of vicious actions and appetites, we cannot
bear God to prohibit our concupiscence, and the more it is
forbidden the more it grows.[22] St. Paul says that in this
way he became a sinner: "Sin was dead, but when the Law
came, it rose up again and grew."[23] The third office of
the Law is to reveal the wrath and judgement of God, who
threatens death and eternal punishment to those who do not
fully observe his Law. Thus Holy Scripture says: "Cursed
is he who does not constantly observe all the things that
are written in the book of the Law,"[24] and St. Paul says
that the Law is the minister of death,[25] and that it works
wrath.[26] When the Law has uncovered and increased sin, and
has demonstrated the wrath and anger of God, who threatens
death, it performs its fourth office by terrifying man.
Then man falls into despair, for he wants to satisfy the
Law but clearly sees that he cannot. His inability makes
him fly into a rage against God, and he wishes that he did
not exist because he fears that God will chastise and
punish him severely. As St. Paul says: "The wisdom of the
flesh is the enemy of God, for it is not subject to the Law
of God, nor can it be."[27] The fifth office of the Law,
which is its proper end, and the most excellent and
necessary one, is that it compels man to go to Christ.[28]
In this way, the frightened Hebrews were driven to ask
Moses, saying: "Do not let the Lord speak to us, lest we
die; you speak to us, and we will obey you and do all
things,"[29] and the Lord replied: "They have spoken exceed-
ingly well."[30] They were praised precisely because they
asked for a mediator between themselves and God, namely
Moses, who represented Jesus Christ, the future advocate
and mediator between man and God. Therefore, God said to
Moses: "I shall raise them up a prophet from the midst of
their brethren like you, and I will put my word in his

mouth; he will say all the things that I command him, and
I will punish everyone who will not obey my words, which
he will speak in my name."[31]

Chapter III

That the Remission of Sins, Justification,
and our Whole Salvation Depends on Christ

Then our God sent that great prophet he had promised us,
namely, his only-begotten Son, so that he might free us from
the curse of the Law, reconcile us with our God, make our
will capable of doing good works, heal our free will, and
restore to us that divine image[32] which we lost through the
fault of our first parents. Since we know that, under
heaven, no other name is given to men by which we can save
ourselves but the name of Jesus Christ,[33] and since he
invites us, crying: "Come to me all you who are harassed
and burdened and I will refresh you,"[34] let us run into his
arms with the footsteps of living faith. What consolation
or joy in this life can be compared to what is experienced
by the man who feels oppressed by the intolerable weight
of his own sins, when he hears such gentle and sweet words
from the Son of God who so graciously promises to refresh
him and to free him from that heavy weight? But the essence
of the matter consists in a true recognition of our infirmity
and misery, for unless one has felt evil, one cannot taste
good. And Christ says: "If anyone is thirsty, come to me
and drink,"[35] as if he wants to say that, unless one real-
izes he is a sinner and thirsts for justice, he cannot taste
how sweet our Jesus Christ is, and how sweet it is to think
and speak about him, and to imitate his most holy life.[36]
     If we know our infirmity through the office of the Law,
then behold John the Baptist points out to us the most kind
physician, saying: "Behold the lamb of God who takes away
the sins of the world."[37] He frees us from the heavy yoke
of the Law, abrogates and annihilates its curses and harsh
threats,[38] restores our free will, and returns us to our

pristine innocence, restoring the image of God in us. As
St. Paul says, just as we all died through Adam, so we have
all been revived through Christ;[39] and let us not believe
that our sin, which we have inherited from Adam, is more
efficacious than Christ's justice, which we have likewise
inherited through faith. It seemed man could grieve that,
without his causing it, he was born and conceived in sin,[40]
in the iniquity of his parents, through whom death ruled
over all men; but now there is nothing to lament, for
similarly without our causing it, the justice of Christ has
come to us, and through him we have been given eternal life
and death has been slain.[41]

St. Paul has a beautiful discourse on these things,
which I want to record here: "Thus sin, and consequently
death, came into the world through one man, and death came
to all men because they all sinned. Although sin was in
the world, it was not imputed as there was no law, yet
death reigned from Adam to Moses even in those who did not
sin in the likeness of the transgression of Adam, who is a
symbol of the future. However, the gift is not like the
sin, for if many have died through the sin of one, many
have abounded far more in the grace of God, and in the gift
proceeding from it, which comes to us from one man, Jesus
Christ. The gift did not come like death from one man's
sin, for the condemnation for one crime led to more
condemnation, but the gift for many crimes led to justification. Whereas one man's sin caused death to reign
through him alone, those who receive the abundance of grace
and the gift of justice for life will reign much more
through Jesus Christ alone. Just as through one man's sin,
evil was propagated unto all men for their condemnation,
so through one man's justification, the good was propagated
and spread unto all men for the justification of life.
Therefore, in the same way that many have become sinners
through one man's disobedience, many will also become just
through one man's obedience. Although the Law intervened
to make sin abound, wherever sin abounds, there grace

abounds much more, and, as sin reigned in death, so grace
will likewise reign through justice, giving eternal life
through Jesus Christ."[42]

Through these words of St. Paul, we can clearly see
what was said above, namely, that the Law was given to make
sin known; but let us recognize that sin is not as powerful
as the justice of Christ, through which we are justified in
the presence of God. Just as Christ is more powerful than
Adam, his justice is stronger than Adam's sin. If the latter was sufficient to constitute us sinners and children
of wrath[43] without any actual fault of our own, the justice
of Christ will be far more sufficient to make us just and
children of grace,[44] without any of our own good works. For
our works cannot be good, unless we ourselves are made good
and just through faith before we do them, as St. Augustine
also affirms.[45] From this one sees that those who lack
confidence in God's benevolence on account of some grave
sins, err greatly. They think that he is not about to remit,
cover, and pardon any immense sin, when he has already
chastised all our sins and iniquities in his only-begotten
Son, and consequently granted a general pardon to the whole
human race. This pardon is enjoyed by all who believe in
the Gospel, that is, in the most happy news which the
Apostles published throughout the world, saying: "We pray
you, reconcile yourselves with God through Christ, because
he who never knew sin has made himself a sinner for us, so
that we may become just in him."[46]

Foreseeing this immense goodness of God, Isaiah wrote
these most divine words, which depict the passion of Jesus
Christ our Lord and its cause so well, that one cannot find
it better described in the writings of the Apostles: "Who
has believed what we have heard, and to whom has the arm of
the Lord been revealed? For he has grown up like a young
shoot in his sight, and like a root from the desert soil,
and he has neither beauty nor decorum. We have seen him,
and his face is not what we hoped for; he is despised and
rejected by men, a man full of sorrows, who has felt our

infirmities and has endured our sorrows. And we believe
that he was wounded and beaten and afflicted by God, but
he was wounded for our iniquity and beaten for our wicked-
ness; he was chastised for our peace, and through his
beating we have become healed. All of us have wandered
like sheep, and each has strayed from the right path, and
the Lord has taken all our iniquities upon himself. He has
been oppressed and injured, but still he has not opened
his mouth; like a lamb he will be led to the slaughter,
and like a sheep that stands mute before his shearers, he
will not open his mouth."[47]

What great ingratitude, and what an abominable thing
it is, if we who profess to be Christians, and who understand that the Son of God has taken all our sins upon
himself, and has cancelled them all with his most precious
blood by allowing himself to be chastised for us on the
cross, still claim that we want to justify ourselves and
to seek the remission of our sins with our own works! As
if the merits, the justice, and the blood of Christ are
not sufficient to accomplish this, if we do not add our own
foul justice, marred by self-love, interest, and a thousand
vanities, for which we should ask God's pardon rather than a
reward! We do not reflect on the threats made by St. Paul
to the Galatians, who were deceived by false preachers;
they did not believe that justification by faith was
sufficient in itself, and claimed that they still intended
to justify themselves through the Law. St. Paul says to
them: "Christ will not aid in the least you who justify
yourselves by the Law; you have fallen from grace, therefore we wait for the hope of justice with the spirit of
faith."[48]

If seeking for justice and the remission of sins
through the observance of the Law, which God gave on Mount
Sinai with so much pomp and glory, means losing Christ
and his grace, what can be said about those who claim that
they want to justify themselves before God by means of

their own laws and observances? Let these people make
the comparison and then decide whether they want God to
give to their laws and constitutions this honor and glory
that he is not willing to give to his own Law.[49] This
honour is only given to his only-begotten Son, who alone has
satisfied for all our sins, past, present, and future by
the sacrifice of his passion, as St. Paul shows in his
letter to the Hebrews and St. John in his first Epistle.[50]
Consequently, every time we apply this satisfaction of
Christ to our soul through faith, we undoubtedly enjoy the
remission of sins, and through his justice, we become good
and just in the presence of God. Thus when St. Paul says
to the Philippians that, according to the justice of the
Law, he had lived irreproachably, he adds: "However, I
decided that what was profitable for me was a loss with
respect to Christ, rather I think that everything is a loss
in comparison with the excellence of knowing my Lord Jesus
Christ; for his love I have considered that everything is
harmful; I have held that everything is dung in order to
gain Christ, and to be found again in him. I do not have
my own justice, which consists in the works of the Law, but
the justice that consists in the faith of Christ, which is
a gift of God, that is, the justice of faith, which allows
me to come to a knowledge of him."[51]

Oh, these are most significant words which every
Christian ought to engrave on his heart and ask God to make
him fully appreciate them! Here you see how clearly St.
Paul shows that whoever truly knows Christ considers the
works of the Law harmful, to the extent that they lead man
away from trust in Christ, on whom he should base his whole
salvation, and they make him rely on himself. Then extend-
ing this judgment, St. Paul adds that he holds everything
dung in order to gain Christ and to be incorporated into
him, pointing out that whoever trusts in works and claims
to justify himself with them, does not gain Christ and
become incorporated in him. Since the whole mystery of
faith consists of this truth, and St. Paul wanted to make

his meaning better understood, he adds and impresses upon
them that he rejects every exterior justification, every
justice founded upon the observance of the Law, and that
he embraces the justice given by God through faith. God
gives justice to those who believe that in Christ he has
chastised all our sins, and that Christ, as St. Paul himself says, "has made himself our wisdom, justice, sanctification, and redemption, so that, as it is written, let him
who glories, glory in the Lord and not in his own works."[52]
It is indeed true that one can find some substantiating
passages of Holy Scripture, which, if misunderstood, seem
to contradict this holy doctrine of St. Paul and attribute
justification and remission of sins to works and to charity.
However, some people have already admirably elucidated
these passages and have clearly demonstrated that those who
understood them in this sense, did not understand them.

Most beloved brethren, let us not follow the stupid
opinion of the foolish Galatians but the truth that St.
Paul teaches, and let us give all the glory of our
justification to the mercy of God and to the merits of his
son, who with his blood has released us from the dominion
of the Law and the tyranny of sin and death[53] and has led
us to the kingdom of God to give us eternal happiness. I
say he has freed us from the command of the Law because
he has given us his Spirit, which teaches us every truth,
and he has perfectly satisfied the Law.[54] He has given
this satisfaction to all his members, that is, to all true
Christians, so that they can appear confidently before the
tribunal of God because they are clothed in the justice of
his Christ, and because he has freed them from the curses
of the Law. Thus the Law can no longer accuse or condemn
us; it can no longer arouse our affections and appetites or
increase our sin, and for this reason, St. Paul says that
the chirograph,[55] which was unfavorable to us, has been
cancelled by Christ and annulled on the wood of the cross.[56]
Because our Christ freed us from the dominion of the Law,
he has also released us from the tyranny of sin and of

death, which can no longer oppress us because they have
been overcome by Christ (and consequently by us who are his
members) through his resurrection. Thus we can say with
St. Paul and with the prophet Hosea: "Death has been conquered and destroyed. Death, where is your sting? Hell,
where is your victory? The sting of death is sin, and the
power of sin is the Law, but let us thank God who has
granted us victory through Jesus Christ our Lord."[57] He is
that most happy seed, who has crushed the head of the
poisonous serpent,[58] namely the devil, so that all who
believe in Christ and place their whole trust in his grace
will conquer sin, death, the devil, and hell, with him. He
is that blessed seed of Abraham,[59] in whom God promised to
bless all nations.

Previously everyone had to fight that horrible serpent
on his own and free himself from the curse, but this enterprise was so difficult, that all the forces of the world
put together could not accomplish it. Then our God, the
father of mercy, was moved to pity by our miseries and
gave us his only-begotten Son, who has freed us from the
serpent's poison, and who has been made our blessing and
justification, provided that we completely renounce all our
exterior justifications in accepting him. Most beloved
brethren, let us embrace the justice of our Jesus Christ,
making it our own by means of faith; let us firmly hold
that we are just, not through our works but through the
merits of Christ; and let us live, happy and confident that
the justice of Christ annihilates all our injustice and
makes us good, just, and holy in the sight of God. For when
God sees us incorporated into his Son through faith, he
will no longer think of us as children of Adam, but as his
own children, and he will make us, together with his legitimate Son, heirs of all his riches.

Chapter IV
On the Effects of Living Faith
and the Union of the Soul with Christ

This holy and living faith is so effective that, whoever believes that Christ has taken his sins upon himself,
becomes like Christ and conquers sin, death, the devil,
and hell. The reason for this is that the church, namely,
every faithful soul, is the bride of Christ, and Christ is
her spouse. We know the custom of marriage, that from two
they become one and the same thing, being two in one flesh,
and the property of each becomes common, so that the
husband says that his wife's dowry belongs to him, and the
wife similarly says that her husband's house and all his
riches are hers. And truly, so they are, otherwise they
would not be one flesh as the Holy Scripture says.[60] In
this same way, God has wedded his most beloved Son to the
faithful soul, and although she possessed nothing but sin,
the Son of God did not scorn to take her as his beloved
bride with her dowry of sin. Through the union of this
most holy marriage, each possesses what belongs to the
other. Thus Christ says: "The dowry of my dear bride the
soul (that is, her sins, transgressions of the Law, the
wrath of God against her, the boldness of the devil over
her, the prison of hell, and all her other evils) has come
into my power and is my property. It is my right to deal
with it as I please, and therefore I want to cast it into
the fire of my cross and annihilate it." When God saw his
Son completely soiled with the sins of his bride, he
scourged him, slaying him on the wood of the cross, but
because he was his most beloved and obedient Son, he raised
him from the dead, giving him every power in heaven and
earth, stationing him at his right hand.[61] The wife likewise says with the greatest joy: "The realms and empires of
my beloved spouse belong to me; I am queen and empress of
heaven and earth. My husband's riches, namely, his holiness,
innocence, justice, and divinity, with all his virtues

and powers, are my property and, therefore, I am holy,
innocent, just, and divine. I am unstained, shapely, and
beautiful because my most beloved spouse has no blemish,
but is stalwart and handsome; since he is completely mine,
all his qualities are consequently mine, and because they
are holy and pure, I become holy and pure."

Thus, beginning with his most innocent birth, Christ
has used it to sanctify the soiled birth of his wife, who
was conceived in sin. The childhood and innocent youth
of the bridegroom have justified the childish and juvenile
life and the imperfect actions of his beloved bride, for
the love and union between the soul of the true Christian
and her spouse Christ is so great that the works of each
are common to both. Thus, when one says that Christ
fasted, Christ prayed and was heard by his Father, Christ
resurrected the dead, freed men from the devil, healed the
sick, has died, risen, and ascended into heaven, one can
likewise say that the Christian has performed these same
works. For the works of Christ are the works of the
Christian, for whose sake he has done them all. One can
truly say that the Christian was nailed to the cross, was
buried, rose again, ascended into heaven, and was made a
son of God, a participant in the divine nature. On the
other hand, all the works done by the Christian are works
of Christ, for he wants them as his own. Because they are
imperfect and he is perfect, and he does not want anything
imperfect, he makes them perfect through his virtue, so
that his wife will always be happy, content and unafraid.
Therefore, although her works are defective, they are still
pleasing to God with respect to his Son, on whom he continually looks.

Oh, the immense goodness of God! What a great obligation the Christian has towards him! No human love is so
great that it can compare with the love of God, the beloved
spouse of the soul of every faithful Christian. St. Paul
says that "Christ loved the church, that is, every beloved
soul, his bride, and offered himself to die on the cross

for her in order to sanctify her, purifying her with the
washing of water through his word, so he could unite her to
himself as a glorious Church--one that would have no stain,
or wrinkle or any such thing, but would be holy and irreproachable, that is, holy and innocent like himself, and
the true and legitimate daughter of God."[62]   As Christ
says, "God so loved the world that he gave his only-begotten
Son, so that whoever believes in him may not perish but may
have life eternal. God did not send his Son into the world
so that he might judge it, but so that the world might be
saved through him, and whoever believed in him is not
judged."[63]

Someone could say to me: "In what way is the union of
this divine marriage made? How is this connection of the
espoused soul with her bridegroom Christ made? How can I
be sure that my soul will be united with Christ and made
his bride? How can I confidently glory in his riches, as
the bride above did? It is easy for me to believe that
others may receive this honour and glory, but I cannot
persuade myself that I may be one of those to whom God
gives so many graces; I know my own misery and imperfection." Most beloved brother, I reply that your certainty
consists in the true, living faith, with which God purifies
hearts, as St. Peter says.[64] This faith consists in giving
credit to the Gospel, namely to the happy news that has
been published by God throughout the world, that
God has used up the rigor of his justice against Christ and
has chastised all our sins in him. Whoever accepts and
believes this good news really has the true faith and enjoys
the remission of his sins; he is reconciled with God, and
from a child of wrath becomes a child of grace, regaining
the image of God. He enters into God's kingdom and is made
a temple of God,[65] who marries the soul to his only-begotten
Son by means of this faith, which is a work and a gift of
God, as St. Paul often says.[66]

God gives faith to those whom he calls to himself in
order to justify and glorify them and to give them life

eternal.[67] Christ testifies to this saying: "This is the
will of him who sent me, that everyone who sees the Son and
believes in him may have life eternal, and I will raise him
up on the Last Day."[68] Likewise he says: "As Moses raised
up the serpent in the desert, in the same way, the Son of
Man must be raised up, so that no one who believes in him
may perish, but may have life eternal."[69] He said to
Martha: "He who believes in me will live, even if he dies;
everyone who lives and believes in me will not die forever."[70] To the crowd of Jews he said: "I came into the
world as a light, so that everyone who believes in me may
not remain in darkness."[71] In his Epistle, St. John says:
"And in this God's love for us was manifest, for God is
love, and he sent his only-begotten Son into the world, so
that we might live through him. The love consists in this,
not that we loved God but that he loved us and he sent his
Son as an atonement for our sins."[72] Moreover, he sent him
to destroy our enemies, and for this purpose he made him
share in our flesh and blood, as St. Paul says, "so that
through his death he would destroy the one who commanded
death, namely the devil, and free all those who were
enslaved throughout their life by the fear of death."[73]
Since we have the testimony of Holy Scripture for those
promises discussed above (and for many other promises,
scattered in various places in it), we cannot doubt that
it is so. Scripture speaks generally, so no one should
fear that what it says does not apply to him.

    Since the whole mystery of faith[74] consists in this,
let us take an example to make it better understood. A
good and holy king has it proclaimed in an edict that all
rebels may safely return to his kingdom because, through
the merits of one of their kinsmen, he has pardoned them
all. Certainly none of the rebels should doubt that they
have really obtained pardon for their rebellion, but they
ought confidently to return to their homes to live under
the shadow of that holy king. If one of them did not return,
he would pay the penalty for it, for he would die in exile

and in disgrace with his king because of his unbelief.
This holy king is the Lord of heaven and earth, who, through
the obedience and merit of our kinsman Christ, has pardoned
us all our revolts, and as we said above, has had an edict
proclaimed throughout the whole world, that we all may
safely return to his kingdom. Accordingly, whoever believes
in this edict will return to the kingdom of God, from which
we were expelled through the guilt of our first parents, and
will be happily governed by the Spirit of God. Whoever does
not believe this proclamation will not enjoy this general
pardon, but because of his unbelief will remain in exile
under the tyranny of the devil and will live and die in
extreme misery, that is, in disgrace with the King of
heaven and earth. This is rightfully so, for we can offer
no greater insult to God than to make him a liar and
deceiver, and we do this by not believing in his promises.

Oh, this sin of unbelief is so grave! Insofar as it
has the power, it deprives God of his glory and his perfection, not to mention the harm of one's own damnation
and the continual torment of the mind that the miserable
conscience experiences in this life. On the other hand,
God is glorified by the man who approaches him with a true
heart in the certainty of faith and who believes in his
promises without the least suspicion, firmly holding that
he will obtain all that God has promised. This man lives
in continual peace and joy, always praising and thanking
God, who has elected him to the glory of eternal life; he
has a most reliable pledge for his most beloved spouse,
namely the Son of God, whose blood has intoxicated his
heart. This most holy faith creates a living hope and a
constant trust in God's mercy towards us, which lives and
operates in our hearts, and through which we completely
repose in God, leaving our welfare to him. As we are sure
of God's benevolence, we do not fear either the devil or
his ministers, or death.

This extremely firm and spirited trust in God's mercy
expands and stimulates our heart, directing it towards God

with the sweetest affections and filling it with most ardent
love. For this reason, St. Paul urges us to go trustfully
before the throne of grace,[75] and he exhorts us not to
throw away our trust, which has a great reward in store.[76]
This holy trust, which never lacks divine love, is gener-
ated in the heart by the Holy Spirit, who is imparted to
us by faith. Consequently, by this living efficacy we are
stimulated to do good, and we acquire so much ability and
inclination for this, that we are most ready to do and to
endure all intolerable things for the love and glory of our
most kind father, God. Through Christ he has enriched us
with such abundant grace and favor, and he had made us from
enemies into most dear children. As soon as God gives this
true faith to man, the force of love impels him to do good
works, and like the best of trees, to yield the sweetest
fruits to God and to his neighbor. In the same way, it is
impossible to set a block of wood on fire without producing
light.

Without this holy faith, it is impossible to anyone to
please God,[77] and by means of it, all the saints of the Old
and New Testaments were saved.[78] St. Paul testifies to
this concerning Abraham, of whom the Scripture says:
"Abraham believed in God and it was imputed to him for
justice."[79] And so he says a little before: "Therefore,
we believe that man is justified through faith without
the works of the Law."[80] Elsewhere he says: "So then, in
the present time the remnant is saved according to the
election of grace, and if it is saved by grace, it cannot
be saved by works, for then grace would not be free.[81]
St. Paul says to the Galatians that "it is evident that no
one justifies himself before God through the Law, because
the just man lives by faith, and the Law does not consist
in faith; but whoever observes what the law commands, will
live by that observance."[82] And he previously says that
man cannot justify himself through the works of the Law,
but only through faith in Jesus Christ.[83] A little further
on, he says that if man can justify himself through the Law,

then Christ died in vain.[84] Comparing the justice of the
Law to the justice of the Gospel, he says to the Romans
that the former consists in acts and the latter in belief,
"because if you confess the Lord Jesus Christ with your
mouth and believe in your heart that God has raised him
from the dead, you will be saved. For one believes in
justice with the heart, and one confesses to salvation
with the mouth."[85] Here then you see how clearly St. Paul
demonstrates that faith makes man just without any aid
from works.

In the fourth book of *On the Epistle to the Romans*,
Not only St. Paul but also the holy doctors who came
after him have confirmed and approved this holy truth of
justification through faith. The chief among them is
St. Augustine; in the book *Of Faith and Works*, in *Of the
Spirit and of the Letter*, in his *Eighty-three Questions*,
in his Letter to Pope Boniface, in the *Treatise on Psalm
31*, and in many other places, he defends this teaching,
showing that we are justified through faith, without the
aid of good works, for the reason that the latter are not
the cause but the effect of justification.[86] He also shows
that when the words of St. James are soundly understood,
they are not contrary to this teaching.[87]

In the fourth book of *On the Epistle to the Romans*,
Origen also defends this teaching, affirming that St. Paul
"means that faith alone suffices for justification, so that
man becomes just through belief alone, even when he has
done no works. In this way, the thief was justified without the works of the Law, since the Lord did not look for
what he had done in the past and he did not wait for him to
do anything after he believed; but, after he had justified
him through his confession alone, he accepted him as a
companion for his entrance into Paradise. In the Gospel of
St. Luke, that notorious woman at the feet of Jesus Christ
also heard him say to her: 'Your sins are remitted,'[88]
and a little later, 'Your faith has saved you, go in
peace.'"[89] Origen then adds: "In many places in the Gospel,
one sees how the Lord spoke in such a way as to show that

faith is the cause of the believer's salvation. Therefore,
man is justified through faith, for which the works of the
Law are no help. On the contrary, where there is no faith,
which justifies the believer, however much man may do the
works that the Law commands, they cannot justify him because they are not built on the foundation of faith; although they may seem good, they lack the faith, which is
the mark of those who are justified by God. And who can
glory in his own justice, when he hears God say through the
prophet: 'Every justice of ours is like the cloth of a
menstruous woman.'?[90] Accordingly, it is only lawful to
glory in the faith of the cross of Christ."[91]

     In his homily, *On Humility*, St. Basil expressly intends
the Christian to consider himself just only through faith
in Christ, and these are his words: "The Apostle says:
'Let him who glories, glory in the Lord,' saying that 'God
made Christ for our wisdom, justice, sanctification, and
redemption, so that, as it is written, let him who glories,
glory in the Lord.'[92] Man achieves the perfect and entire
glorification of God when he does not elevate himself
through his own justice, but recognizes that he lacks true
justice and that he is justified by faith alone in Christ.
And St. Paul glories in despising his own justice and in
seeking through faith the justice of Christ, which comes
from God.'"[93] In the ninth canon of *On St. Matthew*, St.
Hilary says: "The scribes were disturbed that sin was
remitted by a man, for they considered Jesus Christ only
as a man, and that he had remitted what the Law could not
remit, because faith alone justifies."[94]

     St. Ambrose expounds those words of St. Paul: "Whoever
believes in Him who justifies the sinner, has his faith
imputed to him for justice according to the purpose of God's
grace, and David also declares the blessedness of the man
to whom God imputes justice without works."[95] He comments
on them thus: "St. Paul says that whoever believes in
Christ, that is, the Gentile, has his faith imputed to him
for justice, as Abraham did. How then did the Jews think

that, through the works of the Law, they justified themselves in accordance with the justification of Abraham,
since Abraham was not justified through the works of the
Law, but only through faith? Therefore, the Law is not
necessary, as the sinner is justified before God through
faith alone, according to the purpose of God's grace.
Thus Paul says that God has determined that, with the
cessation of the Law, the unjust man should only ask for
faith in the grace of God for his salvation, as David also
said. To confirm what he has said, the apostle gives the
example of the prophet: 'The blessedness of the man to
whom God imputes justice without works.' David means that
those are blessed whom God has determined to justify in
his sight by faith alone, without any toil or observance,
and so he preaches the blessedness of the time in which
Christ was born. As the Lord himself says: 'Many just
men and prophets desire to see the things that you see
and to hear the things that you hear, and they have not
heard them.'"[96]

When he expounds the first chapter of I Corinthians,
the same Ambrose says most explicitly that whoever believes
in Christ is justified without works and without any merit,
and that he receives the remission of his sins through
faith alone.[97] He makes this same point in a letter to
Irenaeus as follows: "No one may glory in his works because no one is justified by his works; he who is just has
justice as a gift because he is justified through Christ.
Thus it is faith that frees through the blood of Christ, so
blessed is he whose sin is remitted and who is given
pardon."[98] In the seventy-seventh sermon *On the Song of
Songs*, St. Bernard also confirms this, stating that our
merits do not have any part in justification, but that one
should completely attribute it to grace, which makes us just
gratis, and in this way frees us from the bondage of sin.
He adds that Christ marries the soul and unifies it with
himself through faith, without the intervention of any
merit from our works.[99]

However, in order not to be too lengthy, I will end these
citations, after I have given a most beautiful thought of
St. Ambrose. In the book entitled *Of Jacob and of the Holy
Life*, this saintly man says that, since Jacob was not the
firstborn in his own right, he hid himself under his brother's attire, adorned himself with the latter's garments,
which gave out a sweet scent, and thus disguised as another
person, presented himself to his father to receive the
blessing for his own profit.[100] In the same way, it is
necessary that we clothe ourselves with the justice of
Christ through faith and hide ourselves under the precious
purity of our first-born brother, if we want to be accepted
as just in the presence of God.[101] This is certainly true,
for if we appear before God without being clothed in the
justice of Christ, we will undoubtedly be judged as completely unjust and worthy of every punishment; but if, on
the other hand, God sees us adorned with the justice of
Christ, he will undoubtedly accept us as just and holy and
worthy of eternal life. Those who pretend to achieve justification by observing God's commandments (which are com-
prised in loving God with one's whole heart, one's whole
soul and one's whole strength, and one's neighbor as one's
self)[102] are certainly very bold. Who could be so arrogant
and half-witted that he dares to let himself believe he has
entirely observed these two precepts, and that he does not
see that, since the Law of God requires a perfect spiritual love from man, it condemns every imperfection? Then
let each man consider his own actions, which seem partly
good to him, and he will find that they should rather be
called transgressions of the holy Law, since they are impure and imperfect actions.

Here those words of David ring out: "Do not enter into
judgment with your servant, for no one living will be justified in your sight."[103] Solomon says: "Who can say, 'My
heart is clean.'?"[104] And Job exclaims: "What kind of a
thing is man, that he should be immaculate, and that he who
is born of woman appear just? Behold, not one of his saints
is immutable, and the heavens are not pure in his sight.

How much more abominable and useless is man, who drinks
iniquity like water."[105]   St. John says: "If we say we
are without sin we deceive ourselves."[106]   And the Lord
taught us that every time we pray we should say: "Dismiss
our debts from us."[107]   From this one can see the foolish-
ness of those who make merchandise of their works, pre-
suming that they can use them to save not only themselves
but also their neighbor.   As if the Lord had not said:
"When you have done all the things that were commanded you,
say: 'We are useless servants; we have done what we were
obligated to do.'"[108]   Here you see that, even if we had
perfectly observed the Law of God, we would still have to
consider and to call ourselves useless servants.   Now,
since all men are extremely distant from this perfect
observance, will anyone dare to glory in himself for having
accumulated so much more merit than the just measure, that
he has some left to give to others?[109]

But, returning to our subject, let the arrogant sinner,
who has done some works praiseworthy in the eyes of the
world, and then pretends to justify himself in God's eyes,
consider that all works which come from impure and unclean
hearts are also unclean and impure, and consequently cannot
be either pleasing to God or efficacious for justification.
We must first purify our hearts, if we want our works to
be pleasing to God, and the purification consists of faith,
as the Holy Spirit affirms through the mouth of St. Paul.[110]
Thus one must not say that the unjust and sinful man becomes just, good, and pleasing to God through his own works,
but one must say that faith purifies our hearts from all
sins, makes us good, just, and pleasing to God, and consequently ensures that our works, although defective and
imperfect, are pleasing to His Majesty.   Because we have become children of God through faith, he regards our works
like a merciful father and not like a severe judge, and he
has compassion on our fragility; he looks on us as members
of his first-born Son, whose justice and perfection take
the place of our uncleanliness and imperfection, which are

not imputed to us and do not come to God's judgment because
they are hidden under Christ's purity and innocence.

Thus it happens that, although our works proceeding
from true faith are impure and imperfect of themselves,
they will nevertheless be praised and approved by Christ
in the general judgment, inasmuch as they are the fruit
and testimony of our faith, through which we are saved.
For if we have loved Christ's brothers, we will clearly
show that we have also been faithful followers and brothers
of Christ, and through faith we will be put in full possession of the eternal kingdom, prepared by our God for us
from the creation of the world.[111] It is certainly not
through our merits but through his mercy that he has elected
and called us to the grace of the Gospel and has justified
us in order to glorify us in eternity with his only-begotten
Son Jesus Christ, our Lord. He is sanctification and
justice for us, but certainly not for those who will not
confess that his mercy is sufficient in itself to make man
just and pleasing to God, who, through his paternal benevolence, offers and gives us Christ with his justice, without
any merits of our own works.

And what can man do in order to merit such a great gift
and treasure as Christ? This treasure is given only through
the grace, favor, and mercy of God, and it is faith alone
that receives such a gift, and allows us to enjoy the
remission of sins. Therefore, when St. Paul and the
doctors say that faith alone justifies without works, they
mean that it alone enables us to enjoy the general pardon
and to receive Christ, who lives in the heart through faith,
as St. Paul says.[112] Christ has overcome the terrors of our
consciences and satisfied divine justice for our sins; he
has extinguished the wrath of God against us and the fire
of hell, into which our natural and acquired depravity
hurled us, and he has destroyed the devils with all their
power and tyranny. These things cannot be accomplished or

done by all the works of all mankind put together. This
glory and power is reserved for the Son of God alone, the
blessed Christ, who has power above all others in heaven,
on earth, and in hell.[113] He gives himself with all his
merits to those who despair of themselves and place their
whole hope of salvation in him and in his merits.

Therefore, when one hears it said that faith alone
justifies without works, he should not be deceived and
think like the false Christians who drag everything down
to the level of carnal life. For them, true faith consists
in believing the story of Jesus Christ in the way that one
believes those of Caesar and Alexander. This kind of
belief is a historical faith, founded on the mere report
of men and writings and impressed lightly on the mind
through established custom. It is like the faith of the
Turks, who believe in the fables of the Koran for these
same reasons. Faith such as this is a human fantasy; it
does not renew man's heart at all or warm it with divine
love, and no good works or a new life follow from it.
Accordingly, they falsely say that faith alone does not
justify but that we need works, contrary to the Holy Scripture and to the blessed doctors of the holy church. I
reply to them that this historical and most vain faith,
with the works added to it, not only does not justify but
also hurls people into the depth of hell like those who
had no oil in their lamps,[114] that is, no living faith
in their hearts.

Justifying faith is a work of God in us, through which
our old man is crucified[115] and we are all transformed in
Christ, so that we become a new creature and very dear
children of God. It is this divine faith which inserts us
in the death and resurrection of Christ, and consequently
mortifies our flesh with its affections and concupiscences.
For since we realise that, through the efficacy of faith,
we have died with Christ, we loosen our ties with ourselves
and with the world, and we understand that those who die
with Christ should mortify their earthly members, that is,

the vicious affections of the mind and appetites of the
flesh. Since we also know that we have been resurrected
with Christ, we endeavor to lead a holy and spiritual life,
like the life we will lead in heaven after the last resurrection. This most holy faith enables us to enjoy the general pardon announced by the Gospel, it introduces us to the
kingdom of God, pacifies our conscience and maintains us in
a perpetual, spiritual, and holy joy. This same faith unites
us with God and makes him live in our hearts and clothe
our soul with himself. Consequently, his Spirit is stirred
towards the same things that Christ was while he conversed
with men, namely, to humility, meekness, obedience to God,
charity, and all the other perfections, through which we
regain the image of God. Thus Christ rightfully attributes
blessedness to this inspired faith, and the former cannot
exist without good works and holiness.

How can it be true that the Christian is not holy, if
Christ becomes his sanctification through faith? Thus we
are just and holy through faith, and for this reason St.
Paul almost always calls saints those whom we call Christians.[116] If they do not have the spirit of Christ, they
do not belong to him, and consequently they are not Christians. If they have Christ's spirit, which rules and
governs them, we ought not to fear that they may become
lazy about doing good works, even though they know they
are justified by faith alone. For the spirit of Christ is
the spirit of charity, and charity cannot be idle or cease
from good works. Indeed, if we want to say the truth,
man can never do good works unless he first knows that he
is justified through faith. Before this, he does the works
more for his own justification than for the love and glory
of God, and so he soils them with self-love and self-
interest; whereas, the man who knows he is justified
through the merits and justice of Christ (which he makes
his own through faith) works solely for the love of God
and of Christ, and not for any self-love or self-justifica-
tion. Consequently, the true Christian (that is, one who

holds himself just through the justice of Christ) does not
ask whether good works are prescribed or not, but stirred
and impelled by the force of divine love, he offers himself eagerly to all holy and Christian works and never
ceases to act well.

Whoever does not experience through his own faith these
marvelous effects, which as we have said, inspired faith
causes in the Christian, may know that he still does not
have Christian faith. Let him urgently ask God to give it
to him, saying: "Lord, help my unbelief."[117] Also when
he hears it said that only faith justifies, let him not
be deceived and say: "Why should I tire myself out in good
works when faith is sufficient to send me to Paradise?" I
reply to him that faith alone does send one to Paradise,
but let him notice that devils also believe and they
tremble, as St. James says.[118] Oh, would you go with them
to Paradise? From this false conclusion, brother, you can
see how much you err; you think you have faith that
justifies, and you do not; you say: "I am rich and pros-
perous and I do not need anything," and you do not know
that you are miserable, wretched, poor, blind, and naked.
I advise you to buy from God some gold made red-hot with
fire, namely true faith inflamed with good works, so that
you may become rich and clothe yourself in white garments,
that is, in the innocence of Christ, and that the shame
of your nakedness, namely the ugliness of your sins, may
not be apparent.[119]

Justifying faith then is like a flame of fire, which
cannot help but shine forth. It is true that the flame
alone burns the wood without the aid of light, and yet
the flame cannot exist without light. In the same way, it
is true that faith alone burns and extinguishes sins without the aid of works, and yet faith cannot exist without
good works. If we see a flame of fire with no light, we
know it is painted and unreal, and similarly, if we do
not see the light of good works in someone, it is a sign
that he does not have the true, inspired faith that God

gives to his elect to justify and glorify them. I believe
with certainty that this is what St. James meant when he
said: "Show me your faith in your works, and I will show
you my faith in my works."[120] He meant that whoever cares
about the ambition and pleasures of the world does not
believe, although he may say he does, for he does not show
the effects of faith in himself.

We can also compare this most holy justifying faith to
the divinity that was in Jesus Christ. Since he was true
man but without sin, he did amazing things, healing the
sick, making the blind see, walking on the waters, and
raising the dead, but these miraculous works did not make
Christ become God. He was God, and the legitimate and only-
begotten Son of God, before he did any of these things, and
it was not necessary for him to work such miracles in order
to become God, but he worked them because he was God. Thus
these miracles did not make Christ become God, but they
showed that he was true God. In the same way, true living
faith is a divinity in the soul of the Christian, who works
marvels and is never tired of good works, but these works
do not make him a Christian (that is, just, good, holy,
and most pleasing to God). It was not necessary for him to
do such works in order to become a Christian, but he does
them all because he is a Christian through faith (in the
same way that the man Christ was God through his divinity).
Thus these works do not make the Christian good and just,
but they show that he is good and just. In the same way
that Christ's divinity was the cause of his miracles, faith
operating through spiritual love is the cause of the
Christian's good works. It was said that Christ had done
this or that miracle, and such miracles not only glorified
God but also were of the greatest honor to Christ as man.
Because he was obedient even unto death, God rewarded him
in his resurrection by giving him every power in heaven and
earth, which he did not have before as man; he had merited
this through the union of the divine Word with Christ's
humanity. Faith works in the Christian in the same way,

for through the union of faith with the soul, what belongs
to one is attributed to the other. For this reason, Holy
Scripture sometimes promises the Christian eternal life
on account of his good works, since they are a fruit and
testimony of living faith, and they proceed from it like
light from a flame of fire, as we have already said above.

This most holy faith embraces Christ and unites him
with the soul, and all three, that is, faith, Christ, and
the soul, become one and the same thing. In this way, the
soul merits whatever Christ has merited, and therefore St.
Augustine says that God crowns his gifts in us.[121] In St.
John's Gospel, Christ himself testifies to his union with
the soul through faith. When he prays to the Father for
his Apostles and for those who would believe in him through
their words, he says: "I do not pray only for them, but
also for those who will believe in me through their word,
so that all may be one, just as you, my Father, are in me
and I in you, and so that they may also be one in us, and
the world may believe that you sent me. I have given them
the glory that you gave me, in order that they may be one,
just as we are one."[122] Accordingly, since we believe the
word of the Apostles, who preached that Christ died for our
sins and was resurrected for our justification, we become
one with Christ, and as he is one with God, so we are also
one with God through Christ. Oh, the stupendous glory of
the Christian, who through faith is allowed to possess those
ineffable things that the angels long to see!

From this discussion, one can clearly see the difference
between us and those who defend justification by faith and
works. We agree in that we also uphold works, affirming
that justifying faith cannot be without good works, and they
say that those who are justified by faith do works which can
truly be called good. We differ in that we say faith
justifies without the aid of works, and the reason is ready,
that through faith we clothe outselves in Christ[123] and make
his justice and sanctity our own. Since it is true that we

are given Christ's justice through faith,[124] we cannot be
so ungrateful, blind, and impious, as to believe that this
is not sufficient to make us pleasing and just before God
without our works. We say with the apostle: "If the
blood of oxen and goats and the sprinkled ashes of a cow
sanctified the unclean with respect to purifying the flesh,
how much more will the blood of Christ, who has offered
his immaculate self to God through the eternal Spirit,
purge our conscience from dead works in order to serve the
living God?"[125] Now let the pious Christian decide which
of these two opinions is more true, more holy, and more
worthy of being preached: ours, which explains the benefit
of Christ and humbles human arrogance, which wants to
exalt its own works against the glory of Christ; or the
other, which obscures the glory and the benefit of Christ
by saying that faith of itself does not justify, and which
exalts human pride, which cannot bear to be justified *gratis*
through Jesus Christ our Lord.

Oh, they will say to me: "Yet it is a great incentive
to good works to say that through them man makes himself
just before God." I reply that we also confess that good
works are pleasing to God and that he will reward them in
Paradise through his mere liberality, but we say, as St.
Augustine also does, that truly good works are done only
by those who are justified through faith, for if the tree
is not good, it cannot bear good fruit.[126] In addition,
those who are justified through faith realize that they are
just through the justice of God executed in Christ, and so
they do not make trade of their good works with God and
claim that with them they can buy justification from him.
Instead, they are inflamed with the love of God and want to
glorify Christ, who has justified them and given them all
his merits and riches; they make every effort to do God's
will and fight vigorously against self-love, the world,
and the devil. When they fall through the weakness of the
flesh, they rise again even more desirous of doing good and
so much more enamored of their God; for they know he will

not impute their sins to them, since they are incorporated
into Christ, who has satisfied for all his members on the
wood of the cross and always intercedes for them before
the eternal Father. Because of his love for his only-
begotten Son, God always looks on them with a most mild
countenance, and rules and defends them as his most beloved
children. At the end, he will give them the inheritance of
the world and will make them conform to the glorious image
of Christ. [127]

It is these loving encouragements that stir true Christians to do good works. When they reflect that through
faith they have become children of God and participants in
the divine nature, they are urged by the Holy Spirit,
dwelling in them, to live as becomes the children of such
a great Lord, and they are ashamed of not maintaining the
decorum of their heavenly nobility. Therefore, they make
every effort to imitate their first-born brother, Jesus
Christ; they live in the greatest humility and meekness
and seek the glory of God in all things; they lay down
their lives for their brothers and do good to their enemies;
and they glory in ignominy and in the cross of our Lord
Jesus Christ. [128] They say with Zachary: "We are freed
from the hands of our enemies, so that without fear we
may serve God in holiness and justice in his sight all the
days of our life." [129] With St. Paul they say: "The grace
of the Lord has appeared, so that we might destroy all
impiety and worldly desires and live with sobriety, holiness, and piety in this world, while awaiting the blessed
hope and the glorious appearance of the great God and
Saviour."[130]

Inspired faith works these and other similar thoughts,
desires, and affections in the minds of the justified.
Whoever does not feel these divine affections and operations
in his heart, either in whole or in part, but is given
over to the flesh and the world, may know for certain that
he still does not have justifying faith. He is not a member

of Christ because he does not have his Spirit, and consequently he does not belong to Christ; and whoever does not
belong to Christ is not a Christian.[131] From now on then,
let human prudence cease attacking the justice of the most
holy faith, and let us give all the glory of our justification to the merits of Christ, with whom we clothe ourselves
through faith.[132]

Chapter V
How the Christian Clothes Himself with Christ

From what was said above, one can understand fairly
clearly how the Christian clothes himself with Christ; still
we intend to speak somewhat more about it, for we know that
the discussion of Christ and of his gifts to the pious
Christian can never seem lengthy or irksome, even if it
were repeated a thousand times. I say that the Christian
knows that through faith Christ, with all his justice,
holiness, and innocence, belongs to him. Just as someone
clothes himself in a very beautiful and precious robe when
he wishes to present himself before a lord, so the Christian adorns and covers himself with the innocence of Christ
and all his perfections. Then he presents himself before
God, the Lord of the universe, relying on the merits of
Christ, just as if he had merited and attained them all
himself. Faith certainly enables us to possess Christ and
all that belongs to him, in the same way that each of us
owns his own clothes. Therefore, clothing oneself with
Christ is nothing other than firmly holding that Christ is
ours (as he truly is, if we believe him) and believing that
this heavenly garment makes us pleasing and acceptable to
God. For it is most certain that, like an excellent Father,
he has given us his Son, and he wants all his justice and
all that he is, can do and has done, to be under our jurisdiction. As a result, it is lawful for us to glory in
ourselves, as if we had performed and acquired these things
by our own powers. Whoever believes this will find without

fail that what he believes is most true, as we have shown above. Thus the Christian should have a firm belief and conviction that all the goods, graces, and riches of Christ are his own; since God has given us Christ, how could it be that he would not give us everything with him?[133] If this is true (as indeed it is) the Christian can truthfully say: "I am a son of God, Christ is my brother, I am lord of heaven and earth, of hell, of death, and of the Law; for the Law cannot accuse or curse me because the justice of my Christ has been made my own."

It is this faith alone that enables man to be called a Christian and one who is clothed in Christ, as we have said, and it can properly be called the great mystery,[134] which contains the marvelous and incredible things of the great God. They cannot penetrate into man's heart unless God softens it with his grace, as he has promised to do through the mouth of Ezechiel, saying: "I will give you a new heart, and I will place a new spirit in your midst; I will take away the heart of stone from your body, and I will give you a heart of flesh."[135] Therefore, whoever does not believe in this way, namely, that he possesses Christ and all his goods, can never be called a true Christian. He will never have a happy and peaceful conscience, or a good mind that is willing to act well; he will easily fall away from good works, or rather he will never be able to do truly good things. This faith alone and the trust that we have in the merits of Christ makes men true Christians, strong, joyous, smiling, enamoured of God, ready to do good works, possessors of the kingdom of God, and his dearly-beloved sons, in whom the Holy Spirit truly dwells.

What mind is so abject, vile, and cold, that the thought of the inestimable grandeur of God's gift to us, the gift of his most beloved Son with all his perfections, does not inflame it with a most ardent desire to be like Christ in good works? For he was also given to us by the Father as an example that we should always follow, moulding our life

so that it may be an image of the life of Christ. As St.
Peter says: "Christ has suffered for us, leaving us an
example so that we might follow in his footsteps."[136] From
this consideration arises the other way of clothing oneself
with Christ, which we can call patterning; for the Christian should regulate his whole life by the example of
Christ and conform to Him in all his thoughts, words, and
deeds, leaving his bad life in the past and clothing himself with the new life, namely, with that of Christ.[137]
Thus St. Paul says: "Let us cast off the works of darkness and put on the weapons of light, not in feasting and
drunkenness, not in fornication and lasciviousness, or in
contentions; but clothe yourself with the Lord Jesus Christ,
and pay no heed to the flesh with its concupiscences."[138]
The true Christian, who is enamoured of Christ, then says
to himself: "Since Christ, who had no need of me, has
regained me with his own blood and become poor in order to
enrich me, I likewise want to give my goods and my life for
the love and welfare of my neighbor. Just as I have
clothed myself with Christ because of his love for me, so
I want my neighbor in Christ to clothe himself with myself
and my goods, because of the love that I bear him for the
love of Christ."

If someone does not behave in this way, he is still not
a true Christian, for one must not say: "I love Christ,"
unless one loves Christ's members and brethren. If we do
not love our neighbor, for the love of whom Christ has shed
his own blood, we cannot truthfully say that we love
Christ. Although he was equal to God, he was obedient to
the Father even unto death on the cross,[139] and he has
loved and redeemed us, giving himself to us with all his
works and possessions. We who are rich and abundant in
Christ's goods should be obedient to God in this same way;
we should offer and give our works, all our possessions,
and ourselves to our neighbors and brothers in Christ,
serving them in all their needs and being almost another
Christ to them. Since Christ was humble, meek, and removed

from contentions,[140] we ought to make every effort towards
humility and meekness and flee all fights and contentions,
those that consist of words and disputes, just as much as
those consisting of deeds.[141]   Just as Christ endured all
the persecutions and disorders of the world for the glory
of God, we should cheerfully undergo the ignominies and
persecutions which false Christians impose on all those who
want to live piously in Christ.[142]   Christ laid down his
life for his enemies and prayed for them on the cross,[143]
and we should always pray for our enemies and willingly
lay down our life for their salvation.

     This is how we follow the footsteps of Christ, as St.
Peter says; for when we recognize that Christ and all his
riches belong to us (that is, when we clothe ourselves with
Christ and become pure and free from all stains), there is
nothing else left for us to do but to glorify God by imitat-
ing Christ and to do the same things for our brothers that
Christ has done for us. Above all, we know from his own
words that he accepts everything we do for his and our
brothers as a benefit for himself. Since we are the true
Christian members of Christ,[144] we can certainly do neither
good nor evil to true Christians without doing the same
to Christ, to the extent that he rejoices and suffers in
his members. Just as Christ is our garment through faith,
so we ought to be a garment for our brothers through spiritual affection. We should also take the same care of their
bodies that we do of our own, for they are the true members
of our body, of which Jesus Christ is the head. It is this
divine love and charity, born in the unfeigned faith that
God inspires in his elect, of which St. Paul says that it
works through charity.[145]

     Because the life of Christ, in whose imitation we should
clothe ourselves, was a perpetual cross, full of tribulation,
ignominies, and persecutions, we must continually carry the
cross if we wish to conform to his life. As Christ said:
"If anyone wants to follow me, let him despise himself and
take up his cross daily and follow me."[146]   The main reason

for this cross is that, by means of this exercise, our
God intends to mortify our mental affections and our physical appetites, so that we may realize in ourselves that
perfection in which we have been embraced by Christ,
through our incorporation in him. God wants our faith,
refined like gold in the furnace of tribulations, to shine
forth in his praise,[147] and in addition, he wants us to
illustrate his power through our infirmity. The world to
its vexation sees his power in us, when our weakness becomes strong through trials and persecutions, and the more
it is attacked and tormented, the stronger and firmer it
becomes.[148] Thus St. Paul says: "We have this treasure
in earthen vessels, so that the magnificence of power
belongs to God and not to us; we endure trials in all
things, but we do not suffocate; we are poor but not
destitute; we undergo persecution but are not abandoned;
we are reviled but do not perish; and we always carry about
the mortification of our Lord Jesus in our flesh, so that
his life is also revealed in our body."[149]

     Seeing that Christ and his dear disciples glorified God
by their tribulations, then let us also joyfully embrace
them, saying with St. Paul: "God forbid that I should
glory in anything but the cross of our Lord Jesus
Christ."[150] Let us behave so that the world in spite of
itself may know and see the stupendous effects which God
produces in those who sincerely embrace the grace of the
Gospel. Let the men of the world see how calmly true Christians bear the loss of their goods, the death of their
children, ignominies, bodily infirmities, and persecutions
by false Christians. Let them see how only true Christians
adore God in spirit and in truth, accepting all that
happens from his hands, regarding all that he does as good,
just, and holy; praising God for all things, favorable and
adverse; thanking him like an excellent and most gracious
father; and recognizing that their suffering, which is

mainly on account of the Gospel and the imitation of Christ,
is a great gift of God. Above all, they know that "tribulation works patience, patience proof, proof hope, and hope
is not confounded."[151] I say that patience works proof,
because God has promised to aid those who rely on him in
their tribulations; this is proved to us when we stand
strong and firm, sustained by God's hand,[152] for we could
not do this with our own powers. Through patience, therefore, we find by experience that the Lord offers us the aid
that he promised in times of need. This, in turn, confirms
our hope, for it would be too great a lack of gratitude not
to expect in the future that aid and favor, which we have
found so certain and constant through experience. But why
so many words? It should be enough for us to know that
through tribulations true Christians clothe themselves with
the image of Christ crucified. If we bear this willingly,
then we clothe ourselves with the image of Christ glorified.[153] Just as the passion of Christ abounds, our
consolation will also abound through Christ,[154] and if we
endure, we shall reign together.[155]

Chapter VI
Some Remedies for Lack of Confidence

Since the devil and human prudence always try to
deprive us of this most holy faith (through which we believe
that all our sins have been chastised in Christ and that
we are reconciled with God through his most precious blood),
it is necessary that the Christian always have his weapons
ready to defend himself against this most wicked temptation,
which tries to deprive the soul of its life. I think that
the most powerful of these weapons are prayers, the frequent
use of holy communion, and the memory of baptism and predestination.

In our prayers, let us say with the father of the
lunatic: "Lord, help us in our unbelief,"[156] and with the
Apostles: "Lord, increase our faith."[157] If we are ruled

by an unceasing desire to grow in faith, hope, and charity,
let us pray continually, as St. Paul commands,[158] for prayer
is nothing other than a fervent desire founded on God.
With the memory of baptism, we become more certain that
we are reconciled with God, for St. Peter says that Noah's
ark was the symbol of baptism. Just as Noah believed in the
promises of God and thus saved himself from the deluge in
the ark, we save ourselves from God's wrath through faith,
which is founded on the word of Christ,[159] who says: "Whoever believes and is baptised, will be saved."[160] This is
very reasonable, because in baptism we clothe ourselves
with Christ, as St. Paul states,[161] and consequently are
made participants in his justice and in all his goods. The
sins we commit in our weakness are covered by this most
precious garment, and they are not imputed to us by God.
As St. Paul says, we feel that blessedness of the psalm
which says: "Blessed are those whose iniquity is remitted
and whose sins are covered! Blessed is the man to whom
the Lord does not impute sin."[162] However, the Christian
guards against taking these words as a license to sin, for
this doctrine does not apply to those who honor themselves
with the name of Christian, and confess Christ with their
words, but deny him with their deeds.[163] It concerns the
true Christians who, although they fight vigorously against
the flesh, the world, and the devil, still fall every day
and are forced to say continually: "Remit our debts from
us."[164] We speak to them in order to console and sustain
them, so that they may not fall into desperation, as if the
blood of Christ did not cleanse us from every sin, and he
were not the advocate and atonement for his members.

Therefore, when we are tempted to doubt the remission
of sins, and our conscience begins to disturb us, adorned
with faith, let us immediately have recourse to the precious blood of Jesus Christ, shed for us on the altar of
the cross and distributed to the faithful at the Last
Supper, under the veil of the most holy sacrament. It was
instituted by Christ so that we would celebrate the memory

of his death, and by means of this visible sacrament would
make our afflicted consciences certain of our reconciliation with God. Blessed Christ made a testament when he
said: "This is my body, which is given for you,[165] and
this is my blood of the New Testament, which is shed for
many unto the remission of sins."[166] As St. Paul says,
"We know that the testament is made by man, yet if it is
authenticated, no one undervalues it or adds anything to
it";[167] and no testament is valid before one's death, but
afterwards it is extremely valid. Accordingly, Christ has
confirmed his testament (in which he promises the remission
of sins, the grace and benevolence of the Father and himself, mercy, and eternal life) by his most precious blood
and by his own death, so that it would be valid. St. Paul
says that, through this act, Christ "becomes the mediator of
the New Testament, so that when his death intervenes for
the redemption of those transgressions committed under the
first Testament, those who are called may receive the
promise of the eternal inheritance. For where there is a
testament, it is necessary that the death of the testator
interpose itself, because the testament of a dead man is
confirmed, while it is worth nothing during the testator's
life."[168] Therefore, through Christ's death, we are
confident and extremely certain of the validity of his
testament, in which all our iniquities are remitted and we
are made inheritors of eternal life. As a sign and a pledge
of this, he has left us this most divine sacrament in the
place of a seal. It not only gives our souls an assured
confidence in our eternal salvation, but it also makes us
secure in the immortality of our body, because from now on
it is enlivened by that immortal flesh, and in a certain
way, it comes to share in its immortality.

Whoever shares in this divine flesh through faith will
not perish in eternity,[169] but if one participates in it
without faith, it turns into a deadly poison for him. When
corporeal food finds the stomach occupied by vicious humors,
it also becomes contaminated and harmful. In the same way

when this spiritual food finds a soul vicious with malice
and unfaithfulness, it hurls it into greater ruin, not
through its own fault, but because to the unclean and the
unfaithful nothing is clean, even if it is sanctified by
the blessing of the Lord. As St. Paul says: "He who eats
of this bread and drinks of this chalice unworthily, will
be guilty of the body and blood of the Lord,"[170] and "he
eats and drinks his own damnation because he does not
recognize the Lord's body."[171] Whoever usurps the Lord's
meal without faith and charity does not recognize the
Lord's body. Because he does not believe that this body
is his life and the cleansing of all his sins, he makes
Christ a liar, he tramples on the Son of God and considers
the blood of the testament (through which he has been
sanctified) as a profane thing; he injures the spirit of
grace, and he will be most severely punished by God for
this unfaithfulness and wicked hypocrisy. He has not
placed his trust in his justification in the passion of
Christ, and yet since he receives this most holy sacrament,
he professes not to place his trust in anything else.
Thus he accuses himself, testifies to his own iniquity, and
condemns himself to eternal death, by denying the eternal
life that God promised him in this most holy sacrament.

At times the Christian feels that his enemies wish to
overpower him, namely when he doubts whether he has attained
the remission of his sins through Christ and whether he can
endure the devil with his temptations. He feels that the
accusation of his doubtful conscience will prevail over
him, so that he begins to fear that hell will swallow him
up and that death has conquered and killed him forever,
because of God's wrath. When the Christian feels these
anxieties, let him go to this most holy sacrament with a
good mind and with trust and receive it devotedly, in his
heart saying in reply to his enemies: "I confess that I
merit a thousand hells and eternal death for my sins, but
this most divine sacrament that I receive now makes me

secure and certain of the remission of all my iniquities
and of reconciliation with God. If I reflect on my actions,
there is no doubt that I know I am sinful and condemned,
and my conscience would never be quiet, if I believed that
my sins were pardoned through the works that I do. But,
if I reflect on the promises and the covenant of God, who
promises me remission of sins through the blood of Christ,
I am as certain of having obtained this and of having his
grace as I am confident and certain that he, who has
promised and made the covenant, cannot lie or deceive.
Through this firm faith I become just, and it is this
justice of Christ which saves me and makes my conscience
tranquil. Has he not given his most innocent body into
the hands of sinners for my sins? Has he not shed his
blood in order to cleanse all my iniquities? Thus, my soul,
why are you sad? Trust in the Lord, who bears you so much
love that he allowed his only-begotten Son to die in order
to free you from eternal death. Christ took on our poverty
in order to give us his riches; he took on our infirmity
to confirm us with his strength; he became mortal to make
us immortal; he descended to the earth so that we could
ascend to heaven; and he became the Son of Man together
with us in order to make us sons of God with him. Thus
who can accuse us? It is God who justifies us; then who
can condemn us? Christ has died for us; rather he has
arisen and sits at the right hand of God, interceding for
us.[172] Oh my soul, then leave off these wailings and sighs;
my soul, bless the Lord, let all that is within me bless
his holy name; my soul, bless the Lord and never forget all
his gifts. He is the atonement for all your sins, he heals
all your infirmities, he rescues your life from death, he
crowns you with mercy and compassion. The Lord is most
merciful and mild; he is slow to wrath and great in mercy.
He does not contend in eternity, and he does not maintain
hate eternally. He has not acted according to our sins,
nor has he punished us according to our iniquities; for,
in accordance with the height of heaven above the earth,

he has exercised mercy on those who fear him; and in
proportion to the distance of the orient from the occident,
he has made our sins distant from us. As the father has
mercy on his son, the Lord has had mercy on us and given
us his only-begotten Son."[173]

It is with this faith and gratitude, with these and
similar thoughts, that we should receive the sacrament of
the body and blood of Jesus Christ our Lord. In this way,
fear is driven from the soul, charity is augmented, faith
confirmed, conscience reassured, and the tongue never
seems tired of praising God and rendering him infinite
thanks for such a great benefit. This is the virtue, the
efficacy, and the unique trust of our soul; the conscience
built on this rock does not fear any storm, not even the
gates of hell, the wrath of God, the Law, sin, death, or
demons, or anything else. Because the whole essence of the
mass consists of this most divine sacrament, when the
Christian finds himself there, he should always hold the
eyes of his mind fixed on the passion of our most gracious
Lord. He should contemplate, on one hand, Christ on the
cross, burdened with all our sins, and on the other hand,
God who chastises him, beating his most-beloved Son instead
of us. Oh, happy is he who closes his eyes to all other
sights and wants to see and understand only Jesus Christ
crucified, in whom all the graces and treasures of wisdom
and knowledge are stored! Happy is he who always feeds his
mind with such divine food and makes his soul drunk with
the love of God by means of such a sweet and saving liquor!

But before I end this discussion, I would first like to
point out to the Christian that St. Augustine is in the
habit of calling this most divine sacrament the bond of love
and the mystery of unity.[174] He says: "Whoever receives
the mystery of unity and does not preserve the bond of
peace does not receive the mystery for himself but a witness
against himself."[175] Accordingly, we should know that the
Lord ordained this sacrament, not only to make us sure of
the remission of our sins, but also to inflame us with

peace, union, and fraternal charity, for in this sacrament,
the Lord lets us participate in his body in such a way
that he becomes one with us, and we with him. Therefore,
since he has but one body, of which he makes us all participants, through this participation all of us must also
become one body, whose unity is represented by the bread
of the sacrament. Just as it is made of many grains,
blended and mixed so that one cannot be distinguished from
the other, in the same way we should be joined and united
with so much harmony of spirit that the slightest division
cannot intrude among us. St. Paul shows us this when he
says: "Is not the chalice of benediction that we bless the
communion of the blood of Christ? And is not the bread that
we break the communion of the body of Christ? Many of us
are one bread and one body, because we all participate
in one bread."[176] Therefore, when we receive the most
holy communion, we ought to consider that we are all incorporated into Christ, all members of one same body, that is
of Christ,[177] in such a way that we cannot offend, defame,
or despise any of the brethren without equally offending,
defaming, or despising Jesus Christ in him. We cannot
disagree with the brethren without equally disagreeing with
Christ, and we cannot love Christ, if we do not love him
in the brethren. We ought to care as much for the brethren,
who are members of our body, as we do for our own body.
In the same way that no part of our body feels any pain
without its spreading to all the other parts, we should not
let our brother feel any pain without also being moved
to compassion.

   With thoughts like these, we should prepare for such
a great sacrament, exciting in our minds an ardent love
for our neighbor. What greater stimulus can incite us to
mutual love than to see that Christ, by giving himself to
us, not only invites us to give ourselves to one another,
but inasmuch as he makes himself common to all, he also
makes all of us one in him? Thus we should desire

and take care that all of us may be one soul, one heart,
and one tongue, harmonious and unified in thoughts, in
words, and in deeds. Let every Christian know that each
time we receive this most holy sacrament, we are obligated
to all the offices of charity in such a way that we do not
offend the brothers in anything and we do not leave anything undone which would aid and profit them in their
necessity. If some who are divided and alienated from
their brethren should come to this heavenly meal of the
Lord, they may know for certain that they eat unworthily;
they are guilty of the body and blood of the Lord, and eat
and drink their own damnation. For it does not fall to
them to divide and lacerate the body of Christ, since they
are divided by hatred from their brethren, that is, from
the members of Christ, and they have no part in Christ.
Yet, by receiving most holy communion, they profess to
believe that all their salvation consists in the participation and union with Christ. Therefore, let us go and
receive this heavenly bread, to celebrate the memory of
the Lord's passion, and by this remembrance, to sustain
and fortify our faith and the certainty of the remission
of our sins; to excite our minds and tongues to praise
and preach the infinite goodness of our God; and lastly,
to nourish mutual charity and to declare it to one
another through the most intimate union that we all have
in the body of Jesus Christ our Lord.

Besides prayer, the memory of baptism, and frequent use
of most holy communion, the best remedy against diffidence
and fear (which is not compatible with Christian charity)
is the memory of our predestination and our election to
eternal life. This is founded on the Word of God, which
is the sword of the Holy Spirit, and with which we can kill
our enemies: "Rejoice" says the Lord "that your names are
written in Heaven."[178] There is no greater joy or consolation in this present life for the Christian who is afflicted
and tempted, or who has fallen into some sin, than the
memory of his predestination and the certainty of being

one of those whose names are written in the book of life,
and who have been elected by God to conform to the image
of Christ.[179]   Oh, it is an ineffable consolation for a
man to have this faith and to reflect continually in his
heart on this most sweet predestination!   Through it he
knows that, even though he may fall, his Father God, who
has predestined him to eternal life, will always sustain
his hand.   Thus he always says in his heart: "If God
has elected and predestined me to the glory of his children,
who will be able to hinder me?"   "If God is for us," says
St. Paul, "who can be against us?"[180]   On the contrary, in
order to accomplish predestination in us, God sent us his
most beloved Son, who is the most secure pledge that we who
have accepted the grace of the Gospel, are among the
children of God elected to eternal life.

This most holy predestination maintains the true Christian in a state of continual, spiritual joy.   It increases
his effort towards good works, inflames him with love of
God, and makes him hostile to the world and to sin.   Who
could be so fierce and ironlike that he would not burn
full of divine love, if he knew that God in his mercy has
made him his child from eternity?   Who could be so vile and
cowardly that he would not consider all the delights, honors,
and riches of the world a most vile corruption, if he knew
that God has made him a citizen of heaven?   True Christians
adore God in spirit and truth; they accept all things,
favourable and adverse, from the hand of God their father;
and they always praise, and thank him as a pious, just,
and holy father in all his works.   Enamoured with their God
and armed with the knowledge of their predestination, they
fear neither death, sin, the devil, or hell.   They do not
know what the wrath of God is, for in God they see nothing
but love and paternal charity towards them.   If they have
tribulations, they accept them as favors from their God
and cry out with St. Paul: "Who will separate us from the
charity of God?   Tribulations, or anguish, or persecution,
or fame, or nakedness, or danger, or the knife?   As it is

written, we die for you every day; we are held like sheep
for the slaughter; but in all these things, we conquer
through Him who loved us."[181] Therefore, it is not without reason that St. John says true Christians know they
must be saved and glorified and that through this trust
they become holy, just as Christ is holy.[182] When St.
Paul exhorts his disciples to the pious and holy life, he
usually reminds them of their election and predestination,
since it is the most efficacious way to stimulate the love
of God and the effort towards good works in the minds of
true Christians. For the same reason, blessed Christ spoke
in public of this most holy predestination,[183] as he knew
that a knowledge of it was very important for the edification of the elect.

     But perhaps you will say to me: "I know that those
whose names are written in heaven have reason to live in
perpetual joy and to glorify God with their words and
works, but I do not know if I am included in that number.
Therefore I live in perpetual fear, especially since I know
that I am very weak and frail with regard to sin. I cannot
sufficiently defend myself from its violence, so I am overcome by it every day. In addition to this, seeing that I
am often afflicted and vexed with many tribulations, I can
almost behold the wrath of God scourging me." Most beloved
brother, I say in reply to these doubts of yours, that you
should believe with certainty that these are temptations
of the devil, who tries in every way to rob you of faith
and of the trust which is born of faith and which assures
us of God's good will towards us. The devil endeavors to
deprive the Christian soul of this precious garment, for he
knows that no one is truly faithful unless he believes in
the words of God, who promises the remission of our sins,
and his peace to everyone who accepts the grace of the
Gospel. I say that whoever is not definitely persuaded by
these promises that God is a favorably inclined and indul-
gent father, and whoever does not wait for the inheritance

of the heavenly kingdom with firm faith, is not truly
faithful and makes himself completely unworthy of God's
grace. Thus St. Paul says that we are the house of God,
provided that we firmly maintain the trust and glory of
our hope until the end.[184] Elsewhere he exhorts us not
to throw away our trust, which has a great reward in
store.[185]

Most beloved brethren, let us make every effort to do
the will of God like good children, and let us be on guard
against sins as much as we are able. Even if we sin
through our fragility, let us not believe therefore that we
are vessels of wrath, or that we are abandoned by the Holy
Spirit, because we have an advocate before the Father, the
just Jesus Christ, who is the atonement for our sins.[186]
Brethren, let us recall that judgment of St. Augustine, who
says that no holy and just man is without sin, and yet he
does not stop being just and holy, provided he regards
holiness with affection.[187] Therefore, if we are afflicted
and troubled, let us not believe that God has sent us our
troubles because we are his enemies, but rather because
he is our most merciful father. "The Lord," says Solomon,
"chastises whomever he loves, and scourges every child
that he receives."[188]

Since we have accepted the grace of the Gospel, through
which God receives man as his child, we must not doubt of
God's grace and benevolence; and knowing that the words of
God and the imitation of the life of Christ delight us, we
must firmly believe that we are children of God and a
temple of the Holy Spirit[189] because these things cannot
be done by the work of human prudence. They are the gifts
of the Holy Spirit, who dwells in us through faith and is
like a seal that authenticates and stamps those divine
promises in our hearts, whose certainty he has previously
impressed upon our minds, and who was given to us by God
instead of a pledge in order to establish and confirm
them. The Apostle says: "After you have believed, you will
be sealed in the promised Holy Spirit, who is the pledge

of our inheritance."[190] See how he shows that the hearts
of the faithful are stamped by the Holy Spirit as by a seal,
in such a way that he calls the Holy Spirit the Spirit of
promise because he authenticates the promises of the Gospel.
This, as we have often said, is the good news that promises
the remission of sins and eternal life to those who believe
that all their sins have been chastised in Christ. According to St. Paul, all of us who believe in Jesus Christ are
children of God,[191] and because we are his children, God
has sent the Spirit of his Son into our hearts, who cries:
"Abba, father."[192] St. Paul says to the Romans: "Those
who are judged by the Spirit of God are children of God.
For you have not received the spirit of bondage once again
in fear, but have received the spirit of adoption, through
which we cry 'Abba, father,' the Spirit himself renders
witness together with our spirit, that we are children of
God, and if we are children, we are also heirs."[193]

One should note that, in these two places, St. Paul
speaks most clearly, not of any special revelation, but of
the witness that the Holy Spirit commonly renders to all
those who accept the grace of the Gospel. If, then, the
Holy Spirit makes us certain that we are children and
heirs of God, why should we doubt of our predestination?
In the same epistle, St. Paul says: "Those whom God has
predestined, he has also called; and those he has called,
he has justified; and those he has justified, he has also
glorified. Then what shall we say to these things? If God
is for us, who will be against us?"[194] If I clearly recognize that God has called me, giving me faith and its effects,
that is, peace of conscience, mortification of the flesh,
and vivification of the spirit, either wholly or partly,
why should I doubt that I am predestined? Then let us say
with St. Paul that all true Christians (that is, all those
who believe in the Gospel) do not receive the spirit of
this world but the Spirit who comes from God, through
whose inspiration they do the things that God has granted

them.[195] Is it any wonder then, if we know that God from
eternity has given them eternal life?

However, some people say that no one should be so
arrogant as to glory in having the Spirit of Christ. They
say these things as though the Christian gloried in having
gained it through his own merits and not through the mere
mercy of God, and as though it were arrogance to confess to
being a Christian. They speak as though one can be a
Christian without having the Spirit of Christ,[196] or as
though we can say, without plain hypocrisy, that Christ is
the Lord, or call God our Father, if the Spirit does not
move our heart and tongue to utter such a sweet word.[197]
Yet those who consider us arrogant because we say that God
has given us the Holy Spirit with faith, not only do not
prohibit us from saying "Our Father" every day, but they
command us to do so. But let them tell me, how can one
separate faith from the Holy Spirit, since faith is the
Holy Spirit's own work? If it is arrogance to believe that
the Spirit of Christ is in us, why does St. Paul command
the Corinthians to examine whether they have faith, affirming that they are reprobates if they do not know that
Christ is in them?[198] Certainly it is great blindness to
make Christians, who dare to glory in the presence of the
Holy Spirit, guilty of arrogance, for Christianity could
not stand firmly without this glorification. But Christ,
who cannot lie, says that his Spirit is unknown to the
world, and that it is known only by those with whom he
dwells.[199] Then let these people become true Christians,
cast away their Hebrew minds,[200] and truly embrace the grace
of the Gospel; they will realize that Christians have the
Holy Spirit and know that they have it.

But perhaps someone will say that the Christian cannot
know he is in God's grace without a particular revelation,
and consequently he cannot know he is predestined. He
could chiefly allege these words of Solomon: "Man does
not know whether he is worthy of hate or love,"[201] and
those of St. Paul to the Corinthians: "I am not aware of

anything, nevertheless, in this I am not justified."[202]
I think that I have clearly shown above, by means of the
words of Holy Scripture, that this opinion is false. It
only remains to indicate briefly that these two passages,
on which the opinion is chiefly based, should not be
understood in this sense.

With respect to the statement of Solomon, although it
is not faithfully translated in the usual version, no one
is so stupid that, if he reads all of Solomon's discourse,
he cannot clearly see that he wants to say: If anyone
wishes to judge whether God loves or hates him by the
occurrences of this present life, he strives in vain,
because the same things happen to the just and the impious,
the sacrificer and the abstainer, the good man and the
sinner. From this one gathers that God does not always
show his love to those to whom he grants external prosperity, and he does not always show his hatred to those whom
he afflicts. Does it seem to you, most dear brother, that
one should conclude that man cannot be certain of the grace
of God because this certainty cannot be understood in terms
of the various happenings of transitory and temporal affairs?
A little before, the same Solomon says that one cannot distinguish the difference between the soul of a man and that
of a beast because one sees the man and the beast die in the
same way.[203] On account of this external accident, shall
we conclude that our belief in the immortality of the soul
is founded only on conjecture? But it is excessive to
weary oneself over such a clear matter.

With respect to the words of St. Paul, I say that, in
speaking of the administration of the Gospel, he says he
does not know that he has made any mistakes, but in spite
of this, he is not at all certain that he has completely
fulfilled his duty, and that in this respect he has obtained
the praise of justice from God, like the person who has
done all that is just and proper for a faithful steward.
In the same way, when a just and discrete majordomo speaks
about his office, he would not dare to justify himself and

maintain that he has completely fulfilled his duty and
the will of his lord, but he would leave the entire
decision to the lord. No one who reads and reflects well
on the preceding and following words will doubt that this
is the sense of St. Paul's teaching. I know well that some
who expound St. Paul's words say that, even though he did
not recognize any sin in himself, nevertheless he did not
know that he was just before God, because, as David maintains, no one can know his own sins perfectly.[204] However,
they do not notice that St. Paul does not base justice on
works but on faith,[205] and that he rejects all his own justice, embracing only the justice that God gives through
Christ.[206] They also do not consider that he was most certain
he would be justified, if he preserved his Christian faith
pure and entire, and he knew that the crown of this justice
was prepared for him in heaven.[207] He was certain that no
creature, whether of heaven, earth, or hell, was strong
enough to separate him from the love of God,[208] and he
wanted to die, because he knew that he had to be with
Christ.[209] All these things would have been false, if he
had not been certain that he was just through faith and
not through works. Therefore, most beloved brethren, let
us cease making St. Paul say what he never thought, rather
what he always most bitterly opposed, for he reprimanded
those who measured justification by works and not by
faith in Christ our Lord.

Other than these two passages of Solomon and St. Paul,
they could cite some other places in Holy Scripture that
exhort man to fear, which seems to be contrary to the
certainty of predestination. If I wanted to explain all
these places in detail, it would be too lengthy, but, in
general, I say that criminal fear is proper to the Old
Testament and filial love is proper to the New. St. Paul
testifies to this when he says to the Romans: "You have
not received the spirit of bondage again in fear, but the
spirit of adoption through which we cry 'Abba, father.'"[210]

He also says to Timothy that God has not given us the
spirit of fear, but the spirit of power and love.[211]
According to the promises made through the mouth of his
prophets, God has given us Christ and freed us from the
hand of our enemies, so that we can serve him without fear
in holiness and justice in his presence all the days of our
life.[212] From this and many other similar places in Holy
Scripture, one clearly gathers that criminal and servile
fear is not proper for the Christian. This is also confirmed for us, in that fear is contrary to spiritual joy,
which is proper for the Christian, as St. Paul clearly
demonstrates to the Romans, when he says that the kingdom
of God is justice and peace and joy in the Holy Spirit,[213]
namely, that whoever enters into the kingdom of evangelical
grace is justified by faith, and consequently enjoys the
peace of conscience that produces a perfect spiritual and
holy joy. Thus St. Paul often exhorts Christians to always
live joyfully,[214] and St. Peter says that those who believe
in Christ rejoice in an indescribable and glorified joy,
even though they are afflicted by various temptations.[215]

Therefore, when Holy Scripture threatens and frightens
Christians, they should understand that it is speaking to
the licentious Christians, who do not observe the decorum of
God's children. These people should be treated like slaves
and held in fear until they taste how sweet the Lord is, and
faith produces its effects in them, and they have enough
filial love to maintain them in the decorum of Christian
piety and in the imitation of Christ. When the same
Scripture exhorts true Christians to fear, it does not mean
that they must fear the judgment and the wrath of God, as
though he were about to condemn them. As we have already
said, they know that God has called and elected them (and
this through his mere mercy and not through their own merits)
because of the testimony that the Holy Spirit renders to
their spirit. Thus, they do not doubt in the least that
through his mercy he will maintain them in the happiness to
which he has called them. Scripture does not exhort them

to servile but to filial fear, namely, that like good sons
they should take care not to offend Christian piety, to
commit any act against the decorum of the children of God,
and to sadden the Holy Spirit, who dwells in us.[216] It
also exhorts us that since we recognize the depravity of
our nature, we should always be attentive and vigilant and
never rely upon ourselves; for in our flesh and mind dwell
appetites and affections that, as enemies of the spirit,
always lay traps for us and strive to make us proud,
ambitious, avaricious, and sensual. It is this fear to
which Scripture exhorts true Christians, who have already
tasted how sweet the Lord is, and who make every effort
to imitate Christ; and as they cast off the old man, they
start to shed this holy fear. However, good Christians
should never completely shed this filial fear, which is
most compatible with Christian charity, whereas servile
fear cannot exist with it.

Through what has been said, one can clearly understand
that the pious Christian does not have to doubt concerning
the remission of his sins or the grace of God. Nevertheless,
in order to satisfy the reader more, I would like to add
some passages from the holy doctors, who confirm this truth.
In the fifth canon of *On St. Matthew*, St. Hilary says that
God wants us to hope without any wavering of an uncertain
will, for otherwise, if faith itself is doubtful, one does
not obtain justification through it.[217] Here you see that,
according to Hilary, man does not obtain the remission of
his sins from God unless he believes without any doubt that
he will obtain it. This is rightfully so, for the man who
doubts is like a wave on the sea, which is beaten and
agitated by the winds, and consequently he should not expect
to receive anything from God.[218]

Let us listen to St. Augustine, who teaches us in his
Manual how to drive out the foolish thought that would
deprive us of that pious and holy certainty: "Let the
foolish cogitation," he says, "mutter as much as it wants,
saying: 'And who are you? and how great is that glory?

with what merits do you hope that you should obtain it?'
I confidently reply: 'I know him in whom I believe; I know
that through his great charity he has made me his son; I
know that he is truthful in his promises, able to give
what he promises and to do what he wishes. If I think of
the death of the Lord, the multitude of my sins cannot make
me afraid. All my hope is in his death; it is my merit,
my refuge, my salvation, my life, and my resurrection.
The mercy of the Lord is my merit, and as long as the Lord
is not lacking in mercy, I am not poor in merit. If the
mercies of the Lord are many, so are my merits; and the
more powerful he is to save, the more secure I am.'"[219]
When the same Augustine speaks elsewhere with God, he says
that he would have despaired on account of his great sins
and his infinite negligences, if the Word had not been
incarnated. Then he adds these words: "All my hope, all
the certainty of my trust is placed in his precious blood,
which has been shed for us and for our salvation. In him
I breathe. Confiding myself in him, I desire to come unto
you, Father, not possessing my own justice but that of your
Son, Jesus Christ."[220] In these two places St. Augustine
clearly shows that the Christian ought not to hesitate but
to be certain of his justification, basing this not on his
own works, but on the precious blood of Christ, which
cleanses us from all our sins and reconciles us with God.

    In the first sermon of *The Annunciation of the Lord*,
St. Bernard says most explicitly that it is not enough to
believe that you cannot have the remission of sins unless
God grants it; that you cannot have any good desires or
actions unless he bestows them on you; and that you cannot
merit eternal life with your own works unless it is also
given to you as a gift. In addition to these things, which
must be considered rather as an uncertain beginning and
foundation of faith, St. Bernard says that you must also
believe that your own sins are remitted by him.[221] Here
then you see how this holy man confesses that it is not
enough to believe in general about the remission of sins,
but you must believe in particular that your iniquities

are remitted by Christ. The reason for this is ready,
namely that, since God promised you justification through
Christ's merits, if you do not believe that you are justified through them, you make God a liar, and consequently
you make yourself most unworthy of his grace and liberality.

You will say to me: "I really believe in the remission
of sins and I know that God is truthful, but I doubt that
I am worthy of such a great gift." I reply to you that
the remission of sins would not be a gift and a grace but
a payment, if God granted it to you because of the worth
of your works. But, I repeat that God accepts you as just
and does not impute your sins to you through the merits of
Christ, which are given to you and become yours through
faith. Therefore, following St. Bernard's saintly advice,
do not believe only in general of the remission of sins,
but apply this belief to your own case, and believe without doubt that through Christ all your iniquities are
pardoned. In this way, you will glorify God by confessing
he is merciful and truthful, and you will become just and
holy in God's sight because the justice and sanctity of
Jesus Christ is imparted to you through this faith and
confession.

Turning now to the discussion of predestination, I say
that, from what has been said above, one understands clearly
that the certainty of predestination does not harm true
Christians, but profits them highly. It does not seem to me
that it can harm reprobates and false Christians, because,
although men so constituted would strain to make themselves
believe that they are among the number of the predestined,
they could never persuade their consciences, which would
always cry out. Yet it seems indeed that the doctrine of
predestination may harm them because they are in the habit
of saying: "If I am one of the reprobates, what do good
works profit me? If I am one of the predestined, I will
be saved without tiring myself out in good works." I
briefly reply to you that, with diabolical arguments like
those, they increase the wrath of God against themselves,

for he has revealed the knowledge of predestination to
Christians in order to make them fervent and not apathetic
in the love of God, alert and not slow in good works. Thus,
on the one hand, the true Christian believes with certainty
that he is predestined to eternal life and must be saved,
not through his own merits certainly, but through the
election of God, who has predestined us, not through our own
works but in order to show his mercy. On the other hand,
he pays attention to good works and to the imitation of
Christ, as if his salvation depended on his own industry
and diligence. But whoever refrains from doing good because of the doctrine of predestination, saying: "If I
am predestined, I will be saved without the effort of
good works," clearly demonstrates that he is not acting out
of the love of God, but out of self-love. Perhaps his
works were good and holy in the sight of men, but in the
sight of God, who looks at his intention, they were wicked
and abominable. From this one can gather that the doctrine
of predestination profits rather than harms false Christians, because it reveals their hypocrisy, which cannot be
healed while it stays concealed under the cloak of exterior
works.

     But I wish that those who say: "I do not want to act
well, because if I am predestined, I will be saved without
my efforts," would tell me why, when they are sick, they
do not say: "I do not want either doctor or medicines,
because what God has determined for me cannot fail." Why
do they eat? Why do they drink? Why do they till the
earth, plant vines, and do all that is advisable to sustain
the body with so much diligence? Why do they not say:
"All these efforts and labors of ours are superfluous, for
is it possible that what God has foreseen and decided about
our life and death will not take place?" Therefore, if the
providence of God does not make them negligent and lazy
in bodily things, why should it make them cowardly and
slothful in things pertaining to Christian perfection,
which is incomparably more noble than the body? However,

we see that the scandal of the reprobates deterred neither
Jesus Christ nor St. Paul from preaching the truth afforded
for the edification of the elect, for the love of whom
Christ was made man and died on the cross. Thus the scandal of false Christians should not hinder us from preaching
predestination to true Christians, since we have seen that
it contains so much edification.

We have arrived at the end of our discussion, in which
our principal aim has been to praise and exalt, in accordance with our limited ability, the stupendous benefit that
the Christian has received from Jesus Christ crucified, and
to demonstrate that faith of itself justifies, meaning that
God receives as just all those who truly believe that Jesus
Christ has satisfied for their sins. However, just as the
light is not separable from the flame which burns of itself
alone, so good works cannot be separated from faith, which
justifies of itself alone. This most holy doctrine, which
exalts Jesus Christ and humbles man's pride, was and always
will be opposed by Christians who have Hebrew minds. But
blessed is he who imitates St. Paul, renounces all his own
justification, and wants no other justice than that of
Christ. Clothed in the garment of this justice, he can
appear most confidently in the sight of God, and he will receive from him the blessing and the inheritance of heaven
and earth, together with his only-begotten Son Jesus Christ
our Lord, to whom be glory for ever and ever. Amen.

8. Camillo Renato, *A Treatise Concerning
Baptism and the Lord's Supper* (ca. 1547)

A. Introduction

One of the most unusual and individualistic figures
among radical Italian religious thinkers was the Sicilian
Paolo Ricci. Born around 1500, he joined the Franciscans
when still young, and seems to have been ordained a priest.
He studied theology at the University of Naples, moved to
Padua and Venice, then left no evidence of his domicile
during the period between 1528-1538. Prior to 1540 he
exchanged his monastic habit for that of a gentleman
scholar and assumed the name of Lisia Phileno.

In Bologna Phileno tutored children of patrician
families, continued his studies, and elaborated his ideas
concerning moral and ecclesiastical reform. After he was
accused of heresy by an Augustinian friar, whose Lenten
sermons of 1540 he had criticized, he found it prudent
to remove himself to Modena. During his stay there under
the protection of the Rangoni and Carandino families, he
came into contact with several religious reform groups
which met in conventicles. In October 1540, he was arrested
on suspicion of heresy and brought to Ferrara for trial by
the inquisition. Phileno was sentenced as a "Lutheran"
heretic to imprisonment, probably for life. He escaped in
1542 and fled to the Valtellina, then a protectorate of the
Swiss Rhaetian Republic.

Ricci-Phileno from this time on assumed a third name,
by which he was known until his death: that of Camillo
Renato. He was employed as tutor as well as preacher by
the noble Paravicini family. Soon after his flight he
established contact with leading Swiss reformers. Heinrich
Bullinger, Zwingli's successor in Zürich, was among Renato's
correspondents for several years. Eventually sharp differ-
ences of opinion developed between Renato and the Swiss,

leading to his excommunication from the Rhaetian Reformed
Church in 1550.

Renato's relations with the pastors of Swiss Protestant
churches remained tempestuous. The chronicle of his
recantations, their suspicions, and his attacks on their
theology and actions (including Calvin's role in the
burning of Michael Servetus in 1553) is long and complex.
Renato spent the remainder of his life under the protection
of the Paravicini. The last certain reference to him, as
old and blind, is from 1572. It is possible that he lived
until 1575 and died of the plague.

Renato's theological opinions defy clear categorization.
He accepted key Protestant positions concerning the sole
authority of Scripture and justification by faith. But he
went on to embrace radical postulates, such as the belief
in the sleep of the soul after death until the last judgment (psychopannychism), or the insistence that sacraments
are only signs. His rejection of infant baptism as practiced by Protestant churches shows his closeness to Anabaptist theology; finally, he was deeply influenced by
rationalist anti-Trinitarian thought.

The treatise translated here is a good example of
Renato's idiosyncratic approach to central theological
issues. It was written around 1547 and addressed to
Agostino Mainardi (1482-1563), a former Augustinian friar,
who after his conversion to Protestantism fled to Switzer-
land, becoming a pastor in Chiavenna. Renato and he had
fierce disagreements about the nature of sacraments.
Mainardi adhered closely to the thought of magisterial
Protestant reformers, while Renato refused to use even the
term "sacraments" when discussing baptism and the eucharist.
For him they were merely signs of what had already been
accomplished by God in the individual soul: the granting
of justifying faith.

Renato's views expressed in the treatise raised serious
questions about the nature of religious authority as well.

His reasoning points to rationalistic individualism in
matters of faith, together with a spiritual conception of
the church as a community of believers rather than a
visible organization.

The verbose and pleonastic style of the treatise confirms Renato's closing remarks that he neither revised
nor polished it. Undoubtedly his arguments could be
understood more easily if Mainardi's tract to which Renato's
is the answer had survived. In spite of the difficulties
presented by the text, the *Treatise Concerning Baptism and
the Supper* remains one of the best examples of Italian
religious radicalism. It is no accident that Lelio Sozzini,
who with his nephew Fausto was the founder of the Socinian
(later Unitarian) movement, based much of his thought on
that of Renato.

The best and most complete work dealing with Renato's
life and religious ideas is George Huntston Williams,
"Camillo Renato (c. 1500?-1575)," in *Italian Reformation
Studies in Honor of Laelius Socinus (1562-1962)*, edited by
John A. Tedeschi [*The Proceedings of the Unitarian Historical Society*, XIV, part I and II (1962-63)], pp. 103-183,
with full bibliography. See also Augusto Armand-Hugon,
*Agostino Mainardo: Contributo alla Storia della Riforma
in Italia* (Torre Pelice: Società di Studi Valdesi, 1943).

The treatise is translated from: Camillo Renato,*Opere,
documenti e testimonianze*, a cura di Antonio Rotondò
[*Corpus Reformatorum Italicorum*, vol. I] (Florence: Sansoni
and Chicago: The Newberry Library, 1963), pp. 91-108.

B. Text

My revered brother,[1] although it is against my inclination to retreat for any reason, especially in matters that
redound to the honor of God our Father and our Lord Jesus
Christ and to the edification of our fellow-men, nevertheless it seems to me that it would have been best to consider

many things before coming to conflicts and arguments
and having our names, yours and mine, talked about in
public; first, because the exposure of our disagreement
makes our weak brethren wonder, and maybe be angry with us;
because the impious will be happy about this controversy
and will use it as a weapon against the faithful, to weaken
the justice of what we profess; then again, because no
one should think that I alone invented and professed opinions which many men here in our community have held and
still hold.

In the second place, consideration should have been
given to the fact that it is the task and duty of all
Christians, and especially the pastors and teachers of the
congregations, to seek that which is useful and edifying
in the Sacred Scriptures, not in the conjectures and
treatises of all sorts of men. Formerly you used to preach
and teach that, in the Sacred Scriptures, and especially
in the New Testament, through the guidance of the Holy
Spirit and the work of the apostles all things were written
which are necessary and sufficient for our instruction and
salvation. And indeed the essential point which makes this
dispute necessary (as you have publicly preached a number
of times, especially on St. James' day,[2] as I hear, and also
the previous Sunday) is not found expressly stated in
Scripture, but is extracted from it, as is also infant
baptism.[3] This is done, so to speak, through skill and
human invention, not the certainty of Scripture, through
conjecture rather than truth; it surely makes us suspect
of curiosity and of wasting our time, and shows us that it
is not necessary for Christians to know something for
which there is no clear biblical foundation, as you say.
It seems to me that the Holy Spirit made the apostles write
about baptism and the Lord's supper as much as suffices for
believing in them and using them. The brief and simple
account of the baptism and the supper seems to be expressly
included and told in the New Testament as necessary and
sufficient for the Christian, because if the matter were as

copious and ample as you and others make it, it would surely
follow that you, living now, possessed greater knowledge and
understanding of the truth than the apostles, as God willed.
Brevity, simplicity, and clarity are requisite for every
science, and especially for Christian knowledge, in order
to be fruitful and conducive to salvation. And furthermore,
if your conjectures, colored and dressed up with a few
biblical passages, should be accepted as necessary by the
people of Christ, it would be tantamount to opening a way
for license and presumption, which would please the papists.

Thirdly, one should consider how much damage was caused,
formerly and now, by the wish to introduce new words not
found in the Sacred Scriptures, and to hold fast to them.
Novelty of words gives rise to novelty of opinions, from
which follow error and finally attitudes inimical to
Christianity. In Holy Scripture, and especially in the
New Testament, the Holy Spirit never used these or similar
terms: "sacrament," "sacrament of the body and the blood,"
but he called baptism "baptism,"[4] the bath of regeneration
and renovation in the Holy Spirit,[5] and the supper "the
Lord's Supper, the table of the Lord, the breaking of the
bread, the fellowship of the body and blood of the Lord."[6]
If the ancients, doctors, or theologians, have used the
former terms, they have not only failed to observe Christian humility, but have without respect applied really
unsuitable names to things. Because the names seemed to be
suitable, they have with too much license further changed
the character and nature of the words, so as to appear to
have applied them fittingly and employed them properly.
This boldness is license and worldly prudence entirely
opposed to the Christian spirit. You will say: "Then one
must not comment on or expound the Scriptures through different words." I maintain that this objection is beside the
point. Though a commentary uses other words, it does not
take away their complete, customary, normal meaning. Calling baptism and the supper sacraments is not appropriate if

the proper meaning of the term should be maintained and
preserved. Many have called the supper a sacrifice; this
is not fitting unless one discards the proper and natural
meaning of the word. I shall not go on with this, so as
not to waste time. I will only say that what is against
Christianity has sprung from innovations of words and
change of the proper and natural meaning, especially in
the treatment of the two subjects of baptism and the supper,
as you can see. Thus, in order to avoid falling into error,
it seems to me that it would be well if we became accustomed,
in these and other matters, to use the names which Holy
Scripture, or rather, the Holy Spirit, has given to baptism
and the supper of the Lord; not strange and foreign names,
as St. Paul admonished us in I Tim. 6 [3-5]. If, then, the
term sacrament and the literal meaning of such a term
are suitable neither for baptism nor the Lord's supper, nor
probably for so many other things to which you apply them,
as I could show you, then such a disputation concerning
sacraments is vain. I do not find in Scripture, reading
it left to right or right to left, that Jesus Christ has
instituted sacraments, for a sacrament, to be exact, is an
oath of obligation, as, for example, taken in antiquity by
soldiers, who swore to serve loyally in war. When a man or
child is baptised or the supper is celebrated, there is neither an oath nor any obligation; they were not instituted by
our Lord for such a reason, or used by the apostles for this
purpose. If you think you should defend the long usage of
such a name and term, that would amount to a defense of
human words, which in every Christian are such as man is,
namely false and lying and serving the devil, in which I
don't want to meddle. Talk ruins the fellowship of Christ;
Scripture establishes it. I want to use here words as a
Christian, not as either a learned or ignorant man. You
call the supper which is celebrated fittingly, as it seems
to you, the sacrament of the body and blood of Christ, not
because of the testimony of Scripture or the aptness of
the term, but only on account of the authority and usage of

theologians both ancient and modern and of human intellect.
Although innovation of words can be tolerated in a body of
learned men, it is otherwise in a sermon, where one does
not dispute with the people, but where Christian doctrine
is taught for the salvation of those who listen. You will
say: "I don't care about the terms; let us call them
signs or seals." I reply that Scripture does not call
baptism or the supper by such names either. You will argue:
"Names should no longer be considered, but rather the
effects." I answer that from the precision of the name
the understanding of a thing arises; if a term does not
suit, the sense of such a term suits even less.

As to the effect of baptism and the Lord's supper, I
maintain and affirm that it is neither the primary nor
secondary purpose of both or either to be seals which confirm and attest. First, because such terms are not appropriate to them, as I have already said; furthermore, one
never finds in Scripture that they were ordained by Christ
to such purpose. If we still want to call them signs
because they signify something, it would be in a general
rather than specific way; this does not mean that they
certify or confirm any more than any other word signifies
the thing that it names. "To signify" means one thing, "to
confirm" another; and frequently, as here, the two are not
joined. You maintain that if they did not confirm or attest,
they would be of no use to those who receive them, as if man
is baptised or partakes of the supper for some sort of profit. For my part, I see no such profit except in words.
Either this benefit belongs to baptism and is always attached
to it, or it is not. If the former, then what advantage did
Jesus Christ gain by being baptised? Did he become confirmed? Did he become convinced of something? I speak of
him as man. Or maybe baptism was less fruitful in him than
in us? What advantage did the nearly three thousand men
converted by the preaching of Peter[7] gain through baptism,
if they were justified by faith? Either they were certain

and clear about justification by faith, or not. If they
were, they could be baptised; if not, they could not at all.
Faith precedes baptism in the adult. And faith already is
firm trust in and certainty of things hoped for and not
seen (as Paul says).[8] By believing were they not certain
of partaking of Christ's happiness and glory, of the remission of sins, and of salvation? Certainly they were!
Being certain follows upon uncertainty, and becoming confirmed upon inconstancy. Unsure man becomes certain, and
doubting man becomes confirmed and constant. Thus miracles
confirm him who doubts and vacillates in his faith.
Miracles give certainty to those who are not altogether
sure. Thus all believers are baptised, whoever does not
believe, or doubts, is not fit to be baptised, much less
to partake of the supper. The eunuch would never have been
baptised by Philip, if he had not believed sincerely and
wholeheartedly; if he had shown a slight doubt about what
was revealed to him, he would never have been baptised.[9]

In what, then, does the child become confirmed, in order
to be baptised? Of what does it become certain? If this
advantage and benefit is the principal and greatest which
proceeds from baptism, why should the child be deprived of
it? And if baptism is like the word, what effect does the
word have in the child who neither hears nor understands?
You will say that the shortcoming lies with the child, not
with baptism. Why, then, do you baptise the child, if it
can not get the chief advantage of baptism, as you say?
And if by chance it were to receive another benefit, then
the one that you consider to be the most important would
not be so; then, in effect, baptism produces such a result
neither in the child nor in the adult. From this it follows
that baptism was not ordained by Christ either primarily or
secondarily for the purpose of making [man] certain or of
confirming [him]. The same thing follows concerning the
Lord's supper. In my opinion, if someone were to show
disbelief or a shadow of a doubt in the remission of sins

obtained [by us] as a result of Christ's death, he would
not be fit and suited to be admitted to the supper because
he does not believe, that is to say, he is not certain
and firm and sure of that which he manifests to believe in
partaking of the supper. An exception to this would be if
you admitted him knowingly so that by taking the supper he
might become confirmed and certain of that which he doubts
and does not believe, which [however,] I imagine you would
never do.

It would be necessary to prove specifically that baptism
and the supper should be properly called sacraments and
seals, not as reckless theologians prate, but by the Holy
Scripture. Since you cannot prove this from the Scripture
in either a straightforward or oblique way, it follows that
the labor [expended on] laying the ground of your belief is
vain and beside the point. Even if your fundamental pro-
positions were true and anchored in the Scriptures (as, in
fact, they are not), you could never completely apply
them to the supper or to baptism, for which truly and properly the name of sacrament cannot be fitting, as I have
said above. Your way of proceeding in this matter (do you
realize it?) is by analogy and not through adherence to
the literal meaning. Analogy has no place where there is
no terminological or effective advantage. If you said that
it is used for description and definition, I would answer
that the definition you gave of the sacraments is sacrile-
gious and scholastic and papal and could not be accepted
either by scholars, who know the true meaning of the term,
or, much less, by Christians, whose peace and contentment
(as Paul says)[10] are in the words of the Holy Scripture of
Jesus Christ rather than in the perversity of papal theologians, who have corrupted the sacred and the profane through
some diabolical design of theirs.

In your first statement you adapt baptism and the supper
to your purpose and say that baptism is preceded by the
promise given by Jesus Christ when he said: "Whoever
believes and is baptised shall be saved."[11] On the contrary,

it seems to me that the promise follows faith and baptism, as for example in the saying: "If you want to enter eternal life, follow the commandments."[12] Eternal life is the reward of faith in the gospel; in the law it is the reward of works. The promise of reward comes after the merit and does not precede it. In speaking of circumcision, God did not say: "If you are circumcised, I shall be your God and the God of your seed," but "I want you to be circumcised as my people so that this sign might show you that you are God's people and that God is your God."[13] It was not said: "You shall be saved and therefore I want you to believe and be baptised," but on the contrary: "You cannot be saved unless you believe and are baptised."[14]

I do not see what promise precedes the supper, which Christ ordered his believers to celebrate in keeping with the meaning of St. Paul who said: "As often as you eat of this bread and drink this cup, you proclaim the death of the Lord until he comes again."[15] We are speaking of the supper which the Lord instituted for his people in later times, not the one which he celebrated with his [apostles]. In my opinion the two are very different in their effect and cause, as I will show you another time. We do not celebrate the supper that he did, but the one that he instituted when he said: "Do this in remembrance of me."[16]

Your second statement seems beside the point to me. First, because you confuse signs and sacraments; I don't see how a miracle could reasonably be called a sacrament, unless the term "sacrament" were to be as general as the term "thing," which suits everything. Holy Scripture preserves the proper meaning of terms and of things and does not apply anything to everything, or one thing to everything, as the papists have done with their mass, which supposedly is good for every evil and for every good. This error arises because it seems that we are ashamed to speak in terms used by Scripture, which in the darkness of this world is an unfailing and clear light of Christians

for speaking and behaving. Another reason [why your
second statement seems beside the point to me is that] you
call baptism and the supper sacraments as if that were
proven and made clear in the Scripture. You will say that
I have a peculiar opinion on this point. I maintain that
this would be the case if Scripture were to say things
your way and I alone contradicted you. But since Scripture
does not say what you and the others do, you must have a
peculiar opinion. The statements of Scripture are reasonable to every pious man; yours are not, especially since,
according to you, they are not proven by the Scripture,
but by discourse and deduction.

The third and fourth statements do not seem to me to be
to the point. Everybody teaches that baptism and the supper
were instituted in the church by Christ. What of this?
Should we maybe conclude that therefore they were instituted
to give certainty or to confirm those who use them? Certainly not. Rather, it seems that according to your fourth
statement, God works something through baptism or the
supper for the benefit of those who receive them, which is
not the case, especially in the supper, which is celebrated
in memory of Christ and of our salvation, but also in baptism [which is performed] in order to show that, as we are
bodily [washed] by the water, so in our hearts we are
cleansed by the Spirit of our evil conscience, that is of
sin, in the name of Jesus Christ. This is not performing
external works; it is showing what God has wrought inwardly
in the believers through the Holy Spirit. Furthermore,
from statements similar [to yours] have sprung superstitions
of the people and errors of theologians, who, thinking that
God employs baptism and the supper as instruments for some
work, have attributed to them a virtue, force, singular
efficacy, and a religion which condemns the ignorant and
persecutes the good and learned Christians. Therefore such
ways of speaking should be sooner held in abhorrence
rather than preached. The devil is subtle, as they say, and
his triumph and victory are the introduction of novelty in

speaking in order to introduce novelty of opinions in the
flock of Jesus Christ our Lord. This should be carefully
pondered. We frequently know the thoughts and designs of
satan, as Paul says.[17]

As for your reasons, they certainly are manifest as
discourses of man, not of Scripture. In my opinion it was
not necessary to adduce the reason for miracles, which are
not sacraments, to prove that sacraments confirm and make
certain, or to put them alongside the supper and baptism,
with which they have nothing to do either in their nature
or in words. But you have already seen the point and that
absence of a proper mutual relationship which would make
you hesitate to use this analogy. Now, in your first
argument, you reason from human signs to the signs of God;
but you do not reach your intended goal through this, because just as many signs instituted and made by men do
not confirm or strengthen those to whom they are made, so
it could be with the signs of God. The insignia and liver-
ies which men wear by the command and wish of their princes
and lords are not prescribed in order to make certain those
who wear them, even less to confirm them, but only in order
to obey their lord and show other men that they are devoted
to certain lords, [as] their subjects or servants, or that
they are of a certain rank and dignity, or belong to a
certain family. It seems to me that baptism and the supper
could be more aptly compared to the latter [kind of signs]
than to the former. Another point is that human signs sometimes are joined to promises so that uncertainty might
become certainty, that doubt might disappear and that imperfect belief might become firmer through the will of him
who promises. This does not apply to baptism and the
supper, which exclude all doubt and disbelief in those who
are baptised or partake of the supper; that is, if they
harbor disbelief, great or small, they cannot or should
not reasonably be admitted either to baptism or the supper.
Then did you not prove, as I said above, that baptism and
the supper are signs of the covenant and promises of Christ,

since it would follow specifically that because the child
about to be baptised is incapable of [entering into] a
covenant or of [making] promises, it should not be baptised,
since it cannot become certain of or confirmed in the will
of God through baptism. And yet we do well to baptise
children in order to show to everyone that they are included in the fellowship of Christians. For this reason I
conclude that the object of baptism and the supper is to
manifest to others the state, dignity, happiness, condition,
mind, love, service, and profession of those who are
baptised or take the supper, rather than to confirm them
themselves in that of which they are certain and sure,
which makes them disposed and able to be admitted to the
one and the other. Since such an effect is commonly seen
in adults and children, it is the principal end, or at
least more important than the one you posit.

As far as your second argument is concerned, which
likens baptism and the supper to the word of God, I maintain that it does not prove what you want, [but] rather the
opposite. Because, as the [spoken] word does not confirm
the man who speaks because he believes what he says to be
true (as Scripture says),[18] but him who hears and maybe
does not believe what is said or believes it only slightly,
so baptism and the supper speak not to him who is baptised
or who takes the supper (since he is sure of what he does
and manifests to be doing), but to those who see and either
don't believe or have doubts about the state of the man who
is baptised or takes the supper. Thus this conclusion is
certain and true and accepted. Your statement that baptism
and above all the supper confirm much more than the word,
since the supper is perceived by more senses, first of all
concludes something which is false, namely that in the
church of Christ the use of the sacraments (as you call
them) is more beneficial and necessary than the preaching
of the Word of God, confirming [the believers] much more
than the Word does, as you say. Thus, it is no wonder that
the papists make frequent use of the mass, having abandoned

the sermon and the Word of God (from which error may God through Jesus Christ liberate his church!). Then, what assurance do the smell of bread and wine and their taste and feel give me concerning things of the Spirit and the will of God, if not that the bread is soft or hard, sweet or tasteless, white or dark, has an unpleasant or pleasant smell? So also for the wine. Such assurances come from our mortal and bodily senses, and so concern corruptible things of this world. This argument of yours is most vain and does not edify the mind, unless you were to throw in some pretty moral, as was the old habit of preachers.

As the word assures and confirms not the speaker but the hearer, so baptism and the supper testify and speak not to the recipient, but to those who see him and are present at such an act. The remembrance of something is not celebrated in order to assure and confirm the man who knows [what] it [is], and who participates because above all he is certain and sure of what he is doing, but to assure those who either do not know the reasons for the action (namely the remembrance), or give it no thought. This is the reason for celebrating the supper in remembrance of the Lord's death and of our liberation, of which we are completely certain before eating the supper. So much so, that if a doubt concerning all this were to occur [to us], not only would we not be confirmed or assured by partaking of the supper, but this partaking would be harmful and damning to our souls, since it would amount to eating vilely and without faith, which is our salvation for every doubt and lack of trust. Thus baptism is an external display, which speaks not to him who receives it, but to those who see it. If the former doubted or did not have faith in some way in the forgiveness of his sins through Jesus Christ and in other matters pertinent to salvation and justification, he would not only not become assured and confirmed by being baptised, but he would condemn himself to eternal death, since he did not believe inwardly that of which he

made an external show. Faith is a necessity [and] must
be in man before he is baptised; it is the possession of
certainty and clarity about that which one publicly
performs. Otherwise woe be to the man who is baptised
or partakes of the supper without being certain of his
salvation through Jesus Christ! Your argument will help
popish Christians, who maintain that a mad and senseless
Turk should be baptised; as they say, it is enough that he
does not object, even if he does not yet have faith and
certainty of salvation. Similarly with the supper, to
which they go without certainty of being in God's grace, or
of having had their sins completely forgiven (the guilt
and punishment, that is), or of having the Holy Spirit.
This is very far from, or rather, contrary to the teaching
of the Gospel. They say furthermore that if a man going to
the supper has no grace, he receives it by partaking of it;
if he has some, he becomes filled with it. These are papal
doctrines originating in human minds, not in Scripture or
the Holy Spirit.

      As to your third point, you first cite Paul's epistle
to the Romans, IV [9], which seems to you to mean that
Abraham was confirmed and assured of his justification
by receiving the sign of circumcision, which according to
you was a pledge of his justification by faith. Not only
you say this, but many give the same exposition. The
contrary seems to be the case to me. Consider it well:
Paul cannot be saying that Abraham was confirmed and assured
of his justification through his circumcision, because
Scripture and the Spirit of Paul testify that before he was
circumcised he was justified for having believed, and not
for being circumcised. Justification is the result of
certain, secure, sincere, and firm faith. Vacillating
faith does not justify, as James says: "He who vacillates
in his belief achieves nothing."[19] And Philip shows it as
well in his discourse with the eunuch,[20] who was not admitted to baptism until he professed to believe with his whole

heart, that is sincerely, as you, too, interpret it. The
heart is not sincere and steadfast if there is vacillation
or disbelief which needs confirmation or assurance. Another
reason [for saying this] is if Abraham was confirmed and
assured by being circumcised, then it was necessary for his
descendants, gentile or Jewish, to be circumcised in order
to be justified and saved. This was the opinion of Christians belonging to the sect of the Pharisees, as it is
written in the Acts of the Apostles:[21] it was not accepted
or commended by Paul. What else did the false apostles
attempt to [establish] by fair or foul means than that
circumcision was necessary either to both the Jew and the
gentile or at least to the Jew? This neither Paul nor any
Christian would have accepted at that time. Then (you will
say) what is Paul's meaning in this passage [Rom. IV, 9] ?
I say that we must be clear about the exact meaning of his
words if we want to understand them without prejudice. Paul
means to prove that there is only one way of justifying
and saving the gentile as well as the circumcised Jew.
He points out Abraham as an example to you, reasoning thus:
the gentile and the Jew are justified and saved in the
same way in which Abraham was justified, who is the father
of the one and the other. Abraham was justified by faith
and by nothing else; thus, the same will be true of his
descendants. Abraham was not justified through his
circumcision, but long before it; much less [will] his
descendants [be justified through it]. The false apostle
will say: "Still, Abraham was circumcised, and therefore
it is not bad for his descendants to be circumcised, so
that father Abraham may be their example." In answer to
this, Paul gives his reasons and says: "If Abraham was
circumcised, it was [through] the will and intention of the
Holy Spirit, who inspired the Scriptures, so that by his
circumcision he might be manifest as father and sure example
to the circumcised of the way of their justification, as
by their foreskin to the non-circumcised gentiles, so that

the Scripture might be fulfilled which says: 'I have made
you father of many peoples'."[22] If, then, Abraham received
the sign of circumcision, it was not a pledge assuring him
of and confirming him in his justification, of which he
was certain and sure and firm, but its purpose was to
certify that the circumcised people, as Abraham's posterity
in the spirit, are also justified by faith like the father,
and not by circumcision or other works of the law, as the
father was not either. Circumcision, then (according to
the meaning of Paul, in my opinion), is not a confirming or
assuring pledge of his justification by faith to Abraham,
but to those circumcised that they are justified by faith
and not by circumcision or works of the law. This should
suffice for now concerning the passage of Paul, which does
not agree with your opinion.

     Your reply to my argument is that the nature and purpose
of the pledge is to confirm. I answer: yes, for the person
who doubts and is not certain. If circumcision is a pledge
(you say), certainly it confirms. Of course (I reply), [it
confirms] him who has had some doubt and infirmity in his
faith concerning the promise of God, because a man who is
certain and sure does not need confirmation. Then, the
words of God to Abraham in this passage are like an agreement and alliance or a covenant. In order to preserve it,
it was almost always customary to add a sign to it, so that
if in the future some doubt should occur, man can be
assured and confirmed remembering the sign. This happens
neither in baptism nor in the supper, which are signs and
outward manifestations of facts in the past, and not of any
promise of future things. Here it would be necessary to
consider the difference that exists between "promise" and
"remembrance." A promise concerns future things, which are
uncertain and doubtful, especially for man. Because of
this it is frequently necessary to add some external,
visible, and durable sign, which might remove future doubts.
Remembrance does not concern future events which have not
yet happened, but those that are past and have already

occurred; and if there is some external sign or act, its
purpose is not to remove doubts to come, but to be a memory
of what has happened. Things past and done have no need of
assurance and confirmation, but future ones certainly do.
Covenants, agreements, and alliances pertain to future,
not past, events. Therefore sometimes *ad perpetuam rei
memoriam*, as it is said, some sign is added to remove doubts
which will occur. It was thus not surprising that God
should have joined to the promises and agreements made with
Abraham, and in him with all posterity, the sign of agreement and union, namely circumcision. But the supper does
not have that purpose or aim, since it is a sign of
remembrance, not of promise, to recall the certainty of
what is past, not to remove some doubt about the future.
Similarly baptism is an action ordained by the Lord Jesus
Christ and performed by the apostles, which shows outwardly
to him who sees it what God has done in us through the love
of Jesus Christ, not what he will do or what he has promised
to do; thus, as water now washes the body outwardly, so
God has washed us inwardly in Christ and through Christ
by the Holy Spirit (who is heavenly water, not of this
world) of all our sins once and for all. I say that he has
washed us in the past, not that he has promised to wash us
in the future. If faith precedes baptism, which it doubt-
lessly does, and is nothing else but the most absolute
certainty and firmest surety in our heart of such a benefit
already received (thanks to Christ), and not to be received
in the future, then baptism is not ordained in order to
make certain and confirm the recipient, but rather to show
outwardly to those present what he has already received
from God through Jesus Christ, and what he is most certain
of having received.

    Circumcision, then, does not resemble baptism; the
former is a sign of the future, the latter of the past.
The reason for my conclusion lies in the fact that the basis
of [your] argument is wrong, [namely] that baptism and

the supper no less than circumcision are pledges of
covenants and promises, and for the same reason. You will
say: "But Christ called wine the blood of the New Testament,[23] that is of the new covenant and new promise made
in the last supper." So you write at the end of your
letter. I answer that in these words of Christ one
should not understand the promise he made to the apostles,
but the second promise and manifest will of God, which he
made before the incarnation of Jesus Christ, written down
and included by Jeremiah[24] in the Old Testament and treated
by Paul in the epistle to the Hebrews.[25] It is as if
Christ wanted to say: "The will of God manifest and declared to the patriarchs was first to accept the blood
of beasts to take away the sins of the people. His other,
second wish was that in future we should no longer be
satisfied with sacrifices made according to the law of
Moses, but with the sacrifice of my blood made once and
for all." Christ, then, did not promise a new testament,
nor did he make a new covenant, but he told those present
and the whole world that he had come to fulfill and satisfy
the second wish expressed by the Father. He stated this
not only in words, but with deeds and actions, and above
all with the symbol of the wine which he poured out. It
is as if our good Lord wanted to say: "As I offer and
pour you this wine for the welfare and enjoyment of your
body, so you should be certain that I shall shed my blood
in accordance not with the old, but, as you know, the new
wish, if you remember God my father, for your benefit,
namely for the remission of your sins and for your joy, not
of flesh or body, but of spirit and soul." This meaning
is gotten from Paul, Hebr. 10, when he mentions Christ who
says the following psalm verses upon entering into the
world: "No sacrifice, no offering was thy demand; enough
that thou hast given me an ear ready to listen. Thou hast
not found any pleasure in burnt sacrifices, in sacrifices
for sin. 'See then,' I said, 'I am coming to fulfill what
is written of me, where the book lies unrolled; to do thy

will, O my God, is all my desire.'"[26] This will is called
the New Testament, of which Christ is the executor and
creator. This new will was indeed the promise of God
made in ancient times to Christ's forefathers and ours, to
which God did not join any sign of the supper or meal, as
is obvious. The supper which we celebrate because of the
order of Christ is not for the purpose of confirming
the promise of the new will of God, but of remembering and
announcing the fulfillment of that will through Jesus
Christ, just as Passover and the eating of the lamb were
only the remembrance of the past and accomplished liberation from Egypt, not for assuring and confirming those who
were eating and who were completely certain of it, but
rather the others, as the Lord seems to point to in this
passage, saying: "And if your children ask, 'What is the
meaning of this rite?' then you shall tell them,"[27] and
so forth. In the same passage God does not call the eating
of the lamb sacrament or pledge, but remembrance: "You are
to observe this day as a memorial of the past."[28] If what
you yourself have preached in the past is true, that the
supper of the Lord succeeds the eating of the lamb as
baptism does circumcision, then you can certainly see that
as the eating of the lamb was ordained in memory of the
past liberation of the people and not as confirmation of
liberation or assurance of the liberated people, so also
the supper is a remembrance of the past, namely, our
liberation through Jesus Christ and his death, and not
a confirmation or assurance of any promise concerning the
future rather than the past. One can clearly see, because
of what was said above, that baptism does not succeed or
resemble circumcision, because the latter is a sign of
the promise and agreement of things to come and baptism
of things past and done. Furthermore, circumcision neither
resembles nor represents that which is promised; but
baptism is very similar to and representative of that which
happened and was already done inwardly, namely the internal

baptism of the spirit by Jesus Christ. The internal baptism of the spirit thus precedes the outward one of the
body. Thirdly, it does not follow that, as before God every
circumcised belonged to the people of God according to the
flesh, so every baptised belongs to the people of God
according to the spirit. Formerly circumcision was a
physical sign of the people of God according to the flesh.
Because of this the gentile was excluded from it and called
uncircumcised, as Paul mentions to the Ephesians.[29]
Baptism is an external sign of the spiritual people of God,
in which the gentile, too, participates in the Spirit, as
Paul mentions to the Galatians[30] and elsewhere.[31] Lastly,
such a simile was invented by men for some sort of purpose.
You will say: "In Paul's epistle to the Colossians[32]
it seems that baptism is called the circumcision of Christ."
I answer that, if it seems so to you, it does not to me,
because Paul speaks in that passage, as also in Romans,[33]
by contrast, that is by an antithesis, as it is called, and
as he does frequently in other passages against false
apostles. Furthermore, baptism shows that the believers
are dead [to sin] in Christ and buried in the spirit with
Christ because of sin, and that they have overcome death
and been resurrected as new men to a new life and state,
which is symbolized by the immersion and emersion performed
in baptism. This reasoning is based on Paul, Rom. VI,
[11]; Col. II, [12]; II Cor. III, [14].

     Circumcision of Christ, then, happens in the soul and
not in the body. It does not physically cut off skin from
the body, but spiritually a bad and deadly conscience from
the soul. This happens through faith and not through
circumcision or any work of the law. We are then the truly
circumcised according to the spirit, and not those who are
circumcised according to the flesh. You find a similar
statement in Romans II, toward the end. In contrast to
physical circumcision, Paul calls this spiritual cutting

off through faith the circumcision of Christ and not of
Moses; in spirit and not in the flesh; in the soul, not the
body; eternal, not temporal; by the hand of God and not
men; secret, not visible; new, not old; pertaining to the
new and regenerated man, not the old man descended from
Adam.   This cutting off, which is nothing else but our
mortification and restoration to life, is symbolized and
represented by our baptism, not to us who are being baptised,
but to those present.   That seems to me to be the meaning
of Paul in the passage of Colossians, until I am shown
otherwise by the words of Scripture, not the constructs of
men.

It seemed reasonable to write you all these thoughts of
mine concerning your tract.   In order to reduce my long
discourse, I should draw it together at this point and
make a summary for your quick orientation.   But I am
deliberately omitting it so that you might be good enough
to take the trouble and ponder carefully at length how
important it is especially for the ministers of the congregations of Christ to consider and distinguish useful and
necessary things from vain and curious ones.   Do not be
frightened by the length [of my tract] which never finishes;
this is due to my large handwriting, as you see, to the
inability of my worldly and physical language to express in
a tract the concept of the heavenly spirit, and finally to
my lack of leisure and time.   But if you were to proclaim
what baptism and the supper are, and to what purpose they
were ordained in the congregation of Christ, I think that
your office would be greater than mine.   You are less
engaged in worldly matters than I; [you should] assemble
all passages of the New Testament where brief or lengthy
mention is made of baptism and the supper and meditate on
them carefully in the Spirit and in prayer.   From them you
should derive a sure and sincere understanding, which should
be sufficient to instruct and teach to the extent to which
it is founded on the expressed and clear testimony of the

Scripture. Scripture (as I have said and as you don't deny) has remained until now through the providence of God, the working of the Holy Spirit and activity of the apostles, a sufficient means of saving and teaching us the necessary, useful, principal, and final things about Christian doctrine and practice. It suffices to protect us from the evil teaching of Satan and Antichrist. It does not need new terms, or new discourses or deductions, or other curiosities, which bring forth contentions and rifts in the flock of Christ. The latter is founded on the word and teaching of its head and ruler, our Lord Jesus Christ. It does not seek to go outside the fixed limits, so that it may not lose its way and be pulled by Satan into error.

NOTES

Chapter 1

[1]Cf. Isaiah, 66, 2.

[2]Cf. St. Gregory the Great, *XL Homiliarum in Evangelica Lib. II*, Homily XXX, in Migne, *Patrologia latina*, LXXVI, col. 1220. Subsequently abbreviated *PL*.

[3]Divisions of the divine office, the public prayer of the Roman church, recited at different times of the day. Cf. art. "Divine Office, Roman," *New Catholic Encyclopedia*, IV (New York, 1967), 917-920.

[4]Cf. Ps. 40, 11, or 101, 10-13.

[5]Originally an office for the night, based on the vigil services of the early Christian church. Since the Middle Ages the service could take place in the evening, especially before a feast day, rather than at midnight or 2 A.M.

[6]Nocturns were prayers which formed part of matins, and consisted of the recitation of psalms, scriptural lessons, and prayers for intercession. Cf. *The Oxford Dictionary of the Christian Church* (London, New York and Toronto, 1958), art. "Matins," 876.

[7]Ps. 50, 129, and 53.

[8]Ps. 50.

[9]Cf. Luke 2, 29-32.

[10]Tacchi-Venturi, *Storia della Compagnia di Gesù*, *loc. cit.*, includes the following note at the end of the articles, which sheds an interesting light on the requirement of secrecy considered so essential by the founders of the Genoese oratory:
"The daughter of Ettore Vernazza, principal founder of the oratory, informs us thus of this unusual practice of secrecy and the purpose behind it:
After his death [of Ettore], I heard that he had done a most secret and very worthy work, which was never found out, although he died in 1524, I think. Then, I believe through the will of God, I just happened to talk with a secular priest, and thinking that he might know something about it, since he was an unusually good man, I said to him: 'I have heard that my father has performed a secret work. If you know anything about it, please tell me.' He answered that he knew the secret, but could not talk to me about it. I

begged him as much as I could. Seeing that I was the
daughter, he told me some things, but not all. 'First
your father had three companions (whom my father chose in
his own way, I believe); one was Giovan Battista Salvaigo,
the second [Nicolo] Grimaldo, and the third [Benedetto]
Lomellino. These four took a house with a garden in a
secret place and started a most devout fellowship which
has grown, and now forty people belong to it.' After the
death of my father five doges of Genoa were elected to it,
and now there are three members of the signoria who belong
to the same fellowship! Nothing about the said fellowship
is revealed: they do their work with such circumspection.
This priest knows everything, because he goes every month
to hear their confession and to give them communion. When
they assemble, they pray for the four founders, beginning
with my father, and say: "May our lord Ettore Vernazza
rest in peace," and then: "May our lord Giovan Battista
Salvaigo rest in peace," and thus they say then for the
other two; but I don't know their first names. I said to
the priest: 'What do they deliberate while they are
together?' He answered: 'I cannot tell you'; but he gave
me a hint, saying: 'The hospital for the incurable has an
income of only ten thousand lire, while twenty-six thousand are spent. In a similar way it is necessary to provide
for the Josephines and women penitents.' Then he did not
want to tell me more. It is enough that I understood that
they deliberated about most excellent things.

    Cf. Donna Battista de Genova, *Vita del Padre et Madre
della R.da M.D. Battista*, in *Opere spirituali*, VI, 9
(Verona, 1602)."

NOTES

Chapter 2

[1]The recipient of the letter is Tommaso Giustiniani (1476-1528). Belonging to an old Venetian noble family, he entered the strict Camaldolese order in 1510 and took the name of Paolo. He was responsible for reforming some of the old monasteries of the order as well as for new foundations, and exercised a great influence over a circle of friends in Venice, among them Contarini, who regarded him as a spiritual model and guide. Most of Giustiniani's writings are only now being edited critically by Eugenio Massa. See his Paolo Giustiniani, *Trattati, lettere e frammenti dai manoscritti originali dell'Archivio dei Camaldolesi di Monte Corona nell'Eremo di Frascati*. Vol. 1: I manoscritti originali custoditi nell'Eremo di Frascati (Rome: Edizioni di Storia e Letteratura, 1967). Also: Jean Leclercq, *Un humaniste ermite: le bienheureux Paul Giustiniani 1476-1528* (Rome: Edizioni Camaldoli, 1951).

[2]Contarini spent Holy Week of 1511 in the Benedictine monastery of San Giorgio Maggiore in Venice, following a common custom at the time. Laymen retired to monasteries on important days of the liturgical year for prayer, meditation, and participation in church services.

[3]Vincenzo Querini was a close friend of both Giustiniani and Contarini. He was born in 1479, and like his friends belonged to one of the great Venetian noble families. From 1505 to 1507 he was ambassador to the court of Burgundy, after having received a doctor's degree in 1502. His learning as well as his attractive personal qualities are frequently mentioned by contemporaries. In 1512 he followed Giustiniani to Camaldoli, became a monk, and took the name of Pietro. Reform of the order and the church were his greatest concerns. In 1514, at the time of his death, Pope Leo X considered making him a cardinal.
No biography of Querini exists. The following articles are helpful in discussing connections between him and intellectual currents of his time: Hubert Jedin, "Vincenzo Quirini und Pietro Bembo," *Miscellanea G. Mercati*, Vol. IV (Vatican City: Biblioteca Vaticana, 1946), pp. 407-424, now also in the author's *Kirche des Glaubens, Kirche der Geschichte*, Vol. 1 (Freiburg: Herder, 1966), pp. 153-166; also "Gasparo Contarini e il contributo veneziano alla riforma cattolica," *La Civiltà Veneziana del Rinascimento* (Florence: Sansoni, 1958), pp. 105-124. Felix Gilbert, "Cristianesimo, umanesimo, e la bolla 'Apostolici regiminis' del 1513," *Rivista Storica Italiana*, 79 (1967), pp. 976-990. James Bruce Ross, "Gasparo Contarini and his Friends," *Studies in the Renaissance*, XVII (1970), pp. 192-232.

[4]A church in Venice which belonged to the Congregation of the Hermits of St. Jerome.

[5]The phrase used by Contarini is: "...lui [Christ] a satisfato ex visceribus charitatis per amor nostro."

[6]Contarini is referring to the War of the League of Cambrai, 1509-1513, which began as a coalition against Venice of Emperor Maximilian, Kings Louis XII of France and Ferdinand of Aragon, and Pope Julius II. Venice suffered territorial losses and military defeat especially in 1509 and 1510. See Felix Gilbert, "Venice and the Crisis of the League of Cambrai," in J.R. Hale, ed., *Renaissance Venice* (London: Faber and Faber, 1973), pp. 274-292.

[7]The letter is addressed to both Giustiniani and Querini.

[8]Contarini left Padua, where he had been studying since 1501, and returned home in 1509. The hard-pressed Venetian republic needed all available resources for defense; expenditures for the University of Padua were stopped, and it was closed from 1509 to 1517.

[9]Psalm 3,2.

[10]Psalm 3,3.

[11]See Psalm 11,7, which Contarini paraphrases probably from memory as was his habit. The modern translation by Ronald A. Knox, which I use throughout, reads: "Patient his [the man's who fears the Lord] heart remains and steadfast, quietly he waits for the downfall of his enemies."

[12]At Camaldoli some monks lived communally, while others lived an eremitical life in small, cell-like huts near the monastery. The hermit to whom Contarini refers was Michelangelo Bonaventura de' Pini, whom he met when he visited Camaldoli in 1515. See A. R. Fiori, *Vita del B. Michele Eremita Camaldolese* (Rome, 1720), and B. Igresti, "I Camaldolesi e il Savonarola," *Camaldoli*, 6 (1952), pp. 138-146.

[13]See Psalm 93, 18-19: "Still, when my foothold seemed lost, thy mercy, Lord, held me up; amid all the thronging cares that filled my heart, my soul thrilled with thy consolation."

[14]Contarini was appointed Venetian ambassador to Emperor Charles V in September 1520. He left Venice in March of the following year, arriving in Germany in April. His first meeting with the Emperor was at the Diet of Worms, after the departure of Luther. Contarini did not see the latter at all, although he knew about him: see Franz

Dittrich, ed., *Regesten und Briefe des Cardinals Gasparo Contarini* (Braunsberg: Verlag von Huye's Buchhandlung [Emil Bender] 1881), pp. 255-6. From Worms Contarini accompanied the imperial court first to the Low Countries and then to Spain. He returned to Venice from his embassy in 1525. His report about it is found in Eugenio Albèri, ed., *Relazioni degli Ambasciatori Veneti al Senato* (Florence: Società editrice Fiorentina, 1840), ser. I, vol. II, pp. 1-73.

[15]Antonio Surian was Venetian ambassador to England from 1519 to 1523. For his appointment see Marin Sanuto, *Diarii*, Vol. 26 (Venice: F. Visentini, 1889), col. 393; his return in November, 1523, is reported by Sanuto in Vol. 35 (Venice: F. Visentini 1892), col. 212.

[16]Here Contarini paraphrases parts of Rom. IV, 6-8: "So, too, David pronounces his blessing on the man whom God accepts, without any mention of observances: Blessed are those who have all their faults forgiven, all their transgressions buried away; blessed is the man who is not a sinner in the Lord's reckoning."

[17]Psalm 38,6: "What is any man that lives, but nothingness?"

[18]2 Cor. I, 9: "Indeed, for ourselves we could find no outcome but death; so God would have us learn to trust, not in ourselves, but in him who raises the dead to life."

NOTES

Chapter 3

[1] For the account of the good thief see Luke 23, 32-43.

[2] Cf. Matt. 27, 46, and Mark 15, 34.

[3] Cf. Acts 5, 15.

[4] Christ in the wine press was a familiar image in late medieval art, and known to sixteenth century readers. See "Le pressoir mystique," in Louis Réau, *Iconographie de l'art chrétien*, II (Paris: Presses Universitaires Françaises, 1957), pp. 421-424.

[5] Cf. Luke 23, 41.

[6] *Ibid.*, 39.

[7] *Ibid.*, 43.

[8] Cf. John 19, 26-27.

[9] Cf. Gen. 9, 22-26.

[10] Cf. Gen. 3, 19.

[11] Cf. note 7.

[12] Caterina Cibo Varano (1501-1557), niece of Popes Leo X and Clement VII, and duchess of Camerino, is a speaker in several of Ochino's dialogues. Besides being well acquainted with him, she was instrumental in obtaining the permission for the establishment of the Capuchin order from Pope Clement VII. She protected the order and materially helped its first foundation near Camerino in 1528. See Roland H. Bainton, *Women of the Reformation in Germany and Italy* (Minneapolis: Augsburg Publishing House, 1971), pp. 187-198, for a biographical sketch and bibliography.

NOTES

Chapter 4

[1]For works by Valdés as well as studies of his thought see bibliography.

[2]See bibliography.

[3]The account of Flaminio's death by his friend Lodovico Beccadelli is translated by Maddison, *Marcantonio Flaminio*, pp. 201-202.

[4]See, for example, the similarity between Flaminio's description of man's love of God "for himself" and that of Valdés, *The Christian Alphabet*, in George Huntston Williams and Angel A. Mergal, eds., *Spiritual and Anabaptist Writers* (Philadelphia: Westminster Press, 1957; the Library of Christian Classics, vol. XXV), 374.

[5]Their names appear on the list found among the papers of Bartolomeo Stella, one of the earliest Roman members; the list was printed in Antonio Cistellini, *Figure della riforma pretridentina* (Brescia: Morcelliana, 1948), pp. 282-83.

[6]For a discussion of older interpretations of Flaminio's religious views see Cuccoli, *M. Antonio Flaminio*, pp. 75-110. For Pole see Paolo Simoncelli, *Il caso Reginald Pole. Eresia e santità nelle polemiche religiose del Cinquecento* (Rome: Edizioni di Storia e Letteratura, 1977).

[7]Cf., for example, Rom. 12, 12; Eph. 6, 18; Phil. 4, 6; Col. 4, 2.

[8]Flaminio draws here on Rom. 6, 3-11.

[9]Rom. 8, 9.

NOTES

Chapter 5

[1]The Franciscan Brother Bonaventura, provincial of his
order, was deeply concerned with ecclesiastical and monastic
reform. For bibliography see *Concilium Tridentinum*,
Vol. XII (Freiburg im Breisgau: Herder, 1929), p. 67,
n. 3.

[2]Carafa's sister Maria became a Dominican nun in 1490,
and with his aid and encouragement was active in reforming
the Neapolitan branch of her order. See Ludwig von Pastor,
*The History of the Popes from the Closing of the Middle
Ages*, Vol. X (St. Louis and London: Herder, 1910), p. 420.

[3]Hebr. 11, 6.

[4]Carafa uses the term "apostates" throughout the
memorial to indicate monks or friars who have made the
solemn vows of poverty, chastity, and obedience, but
subsequently left their orders without permission of their
superiors. Conventuals were members of conventual, i.e.
unreformed branches of their orders. The term is used most
commonly in connection with the Franciscan order, in which
repeatedly groups of monasteries joined together to observe
more strictly the rule of St. Francis, and were called
"observants." Eventually they became a separate order of
Franciscans, recognized as such by the bull *Ite vos* of
Pope Leo X of May 30, 1517. See John Moorman, *A History of
the Franciscan Order* (Oxford: Clarendon Press, 1968), pp.
582-585.

[5]Girolamo Galateo (ca. 1490-1541), Franciscan theologian, at Carafa's instigation was imprisoned on suspicion
of heresy, tried in 1530 and condemned to death. The
Venetian authorities did not allow the sentence to be
executed. After seven years in prison Galateo was briefly
released, then thrown in prison again, where he died. See
Karl Benrath, *Geschichte der Reformation in Venedig* (Halle:
Verein für Reformationsgeschichte, 1887), pp. 8-9. G. K.
Brown, *Italy and the Reformation* (Oxford: Blackwell, 1933),
p. 125, calls Galateo a Lutheran. Still useful is E. Comba,
I nostri Protestanti (Florence: Claudiana, 1897), Vol. II,
pp. 51-81. For more recent bibliography, see R. Freschi,
"Girolamo Galateo e la sua Apologia," *Studi e materiali di
storia delle religioni*, Vol. XI (1935), pp. 96-97, and a
brief discussion by Aldo Stella, *Anabattismo e Antitrinitarismo in Italia nel XVI Secolo* (Padua: Liviana Editrice,
1969), pp. 105-109.

[6]Bartolomeo Fonzio, Venetian Franciscan, came to
Carafa's notice as a result of preaching a suspect sermon
in 1529. Forbidden to continue preaching by a papal brief,
Fonzio a year later fled to Germany. He obtained release
from his monastic vows and returned to Italy, where he was
active as a teacher until his imprisonment by the Venetian
Inquisition in 1558. He was found guilty of heresy and
executed by being drowned in 1562. See Benrath, *Geschichte
der Reformation in Venedig*, pp. 12-13, and 62-66. Achille
Olivieri, "Il 'Cathechismo' e la 'Fidei et doctrinae . . .
ratio' di Bartolomeo Fonzio eretico veneziano del Cinquecento," *Studi Veneziani*, Vol. IX (1967), pp. 339-452.
Stella, *Anabattismo*, pp. 107-110.

[7]The papal legate in Venice from 1517-1531 was Alto-
bellus Averoldus, bishop of Pola. See Pius Bonifatius Gams,
Series episcoporum Ecclesiae catholicae (Regensburg: Manz,
1873), p. 803.

[8]Jacopo Salviati, the husband of Lucrezia de'Medici
(sister of Pope Leo X), was a confidant of Pope Clement
VII, who frequently used him as secretary, envoy, or nego-
tiator in political and diplomatic affairs. See Pastor,
History of the Popes, Vols. IX and X, *passim*.

[9]Little is known about Alessandro Pagliarino of Pieve
di Sacco, another Franciscan. He apparently regained his
liberty after the date of Carafa's memorial, since he was
imprisoned again in 1540 and escaped with the help of an
influential Venetian patrician, Francesco Contarini,
relative of Cardinal Gasparo Contarini. See Stella,
Anabattismo, p. 107.

[10]Unclear reference.

[11]Martin of Treviso was minister of the Venetian province of Conventual Franciscans: *Concilium Tridentinum*
Vol. XII, p. 68, n. 5.

[12]Pope Nicholas V in 1451 amalgamated the bishopric of
Venice (Castello) and the ancient patriarchate of Grado.
Henceforth the title of patriarch passed to the highest
ecclesiastical official of Venice. See Antonio Niero,
I Patriarchi di Venezia (Venice: Studium cattolico
veneziano, 1961), p. 9.

[13]Rom. 2, 24.

[14]The Sacred Penitentiary is one of the tribunals of the
Holy See. It is empowered to deal with matters of conscience
("the internal forum") and to grant indulgences. Cases
coming before it include matters involving absolutions,
dispensations, and religious vows or promises. For its

history, organization, and further bibliography, see the
New Catholic Encyclopedia, Vol. XI, pp. 87-88. For the
sixteenth century see Emil Göller, *Die päpstliche
Pönitentiarie von ihrem Ursprung bis zu ihrer Umgestaltung
unter Pius V*, 2 vols. (Rome: Loescher, 1907-1911).

[15]Twenty-one years for ordination to the sub-deaconate;
twenty-two for the deaconate; twenty-four (or twenty-three
with dispensation) for the priesthood. See *Dictionnaire du
Droit Canonique*, Vol. VI, p. 1126.

[16]See Isaiah 28, 19.

[17]Lorenzo Pucci, member of a Florentine family connected with the Medici, was cardinal and grand-penitentiary
under Pope Leo X. He was often called "Card. Quattro
Coronati" after his titular church. He resigned his office
to his nephew in 1529 and died in 1531. Antonio Pucci,
nephew of Lorenzo, not only succeeded him in office, but
became cardinal priest of the same church, Santi Quattro
Coronati. See Göller, *Die päpstliche Pönitentiarie*, Vol.
II, p. 11.

[18]A reference to Lorenzo Pucci?

[19]Matt. 9, 17.

[20]Mark 2, 22.

[21]Giving and receiving a church or abbey *in commendam*
(in trust) was a temporary arrangement which became common
in the early Middle Ages. The recipient was not fully or
not at all qualified to exercise the office attached to the
benefice, but could draw the income from it (for example,
a layman who received an abbey *in commendam*). For primarily
financial reasons these grants persisted as one of the most
flagrant abuses in the late medieval church, and could
still be found in the eighteenth and nineteenth centuries.
See the article "Commende" in *Dictionnaire du Droit Canonique*, Vol. III, pp. 1029-1085, and *New Catholic Encyclopedia*,
vol. IV, p. 9.

[22]Ps. 106, 18.

[23]In 1524 Clement VII issued a number of directives
concerning reform of the secular clergy. One of his briefs,
to which reference is made here, was directed to Carafa,
and aimed at suppression of simony. See Pastor, *History of
the Popes*, Vol. X, pp. 380-381.

[24]Joannes Rosa was bishop of Veglia from 1531 to 1550
(today the island of Krk off the Dalmatian coast in
Yugoslavia), which belonged to Venice in the sixteenth
century. See Conrad Eubel, *Hierarchia Catholica Medii
Aevi*, Vol. III (Münster: Regensberg, 1923), p. 328.

[25]A pun on the name of the diocese, Veglia, and the
Italian verb "vegliare," meaning to watch.

[26]Girolamo Querini, patriarch of Venice from 1524-1554,
repeatedly clashed with the Venetian government over
jurisdictional issues and was absent from his see for long
periods of time. See Niero, *I Patriarchi di Venezia*, pp.
72-87.

[27]Gianmatteo Giberti, one of the signers of the
Consilium de emendanda Ecclesia, was bishop of Verona from
1524 to 1543. The best work on him is Adriano Prosperi,
Tra evangelismo e controriforma: G. M. Giberti (1495-1543)
(Rome: Edizioni di Storia e Letteratura, 1969). Still useful is M. A. Tucker, "Gian Matteo Giberti, Papal Politician
and Catholic Reformer," *English Historical Review*, Vol. 18
(1903), pp. 24-51, 266-286, and 439-469.

[28]In this and the following sentences Carafa loosely
quotes several biblical passages. Cf. Jeremiah 11, 1.

[29]Deut. 32, 36.

[30]Ps. 79, 13.

[31]Micah 7, 1.

[32]The Observant Franciscans.

[33]Territorial division of a religious order, formed by
the union of individually administered monasteries under
one common superior. The pope has final authority over
religious provinces. See the *New Catholic Encyclopedia*,
Vol. XI, pp. 923-924 for fuller discussion and bibliography.

[34]Cf. Acts 4, 32.

[35]See P. E. d'Alençon, "Gian Pietro Caraffa, vescovo
di Chieti (Paolo IV) e la riforma dell'Ordine dei Minori
dell'Osservanza," *Miscellanea Franciscana*, Vol. 13 (1911).

[36]Eugenius IV was pope from 1431 to 1447. His bull
Ut sacra of January 11, 1446 gave the Observant Franciscans
a large measure of independence from Conventual Franciscans.
They could hold their own general chapters and promulgate
their own legislation. See Moorman, *A History of the
Franciscan Order*, p. 452.

[37]Mal. 2, 14.

[38]Like the Observant. Franciscans, the Capuchins grew
out of a move to reform the order. Founded by Matteo da
Bascio in 1525, they became a recognized religious congregation on July 3, 1528, when Pope Clement VII issued the
bull *Religionis zelus*, and were approved as a separate
order by Pope Paul III in 1536. Their original name was
Friars Minor of the Eremitical Life; the term Capuchins
was the popular name given them on account of the simple
habit and form of the hood ("cappuccio") which they wore.
The order distinguished itself by the strict observance
of the Franciscan rule and charitable as well as missionary
work among the poor. For histories of the order see
Melchior a Pobladura, *Historia generalis Ordinis Fratrum
Minorum Capuchinorum*, 3 vols. in 4 (Rome: Institutum
historicum Ordinis Fratrum Minorum Capuchinorum, 1947-1951),
and Father Cuthbert, *The Capuchins: a Contribution to the
History of the Counter-Reformation*, 2 Vols. (London: Sheed
and Ward, 1928).

[39]Ps. 144, 19.

[40]Matt. 11, 12.

[41]The cardinal protector of the Franciscan order in
1532, the date of Carafa's memorial, was Cardinal Andreas
de Valle. See Heribert Holzapfel, *The History of the
Franciscan Order* (Teutopolis, Ill.: St. Joseph Seminary,
1948).

[42]Both orders were founded during the crusades in the
twelfth century and attempted to combine the chivalric and
monastic ideals. The Order of the Hospital of St. John of
Jerusalem (later called the Knights of Malta), as its name
implies, originally devoted itself to the care of sick
pilgrims and crusaders. The second order mentioned by
Carafa is better known under the name of Teutonic Knights.
Its members were active both in the crusades in the Holy
Land and the colonization of eastern Germany, where they
played a significant role. For a recent sketch of the
history of both orders and especially for further bibliography see Desmond Seward, *The Monks of War: the Military
Religious Orders* (Hamden, Conn.: Archon Books, 1972).

[43]Especially important in the history of the Spanish
struggles with the Moors were the military orders of
Calatrava, Alcántara, and Santiago. In addition to Seward,
The Monks of War, see Georgiana Goddard King, *A Brief
Account of the Military Orders in Spain* (New York: The
Hispanic Society, 1921).

[44]St. Dominic (ca. 1170-1221) founded the Order of
Friars Preachers, better known as Dominicans. They were
approved by Pope Honorius III in 1216 and 1217; their
primary purpose was preaching against Albigensian heretics

and missionary work. Among the voluminous literature see
especially Marie Humbert Vicaire, *Saint Dominic and His
Times* (New York: McGraw-Hill, 1964).

[45]Cf. Ps. 90, 7.

[46]The Knights of Malta held the island of Rhodes from
1310 to 1522, when they lost it to the victorious Ottoman
Turks. See Seward, *The Monks of War*, pp. 215-254.

[47]Margrave Albrecht of Brandenburg, grand master of
the order in 1512, became a Lutheran. *Ibid.*, p. 128.

[48]Probably Andrea Lippomano, who belonged to the
Teutonic Knights, and whose plan for reform of the order
Carafa seems to sketch here. See Silvio Tramontin, "Lo
spirito, le attività, gli sviluppi dell'Oratorio del
Divino Amore nella Venezia del Cinquecento," *Studi Veneziani*,
Vol. XIV (1972), p. 128.

NOTES

Chapter 6

[1]Cf. Psalm 32, 6.

[2]*On the Gospel of John, PL,* Vol. 35, col. 1425.

[3]Cf. 2 Tim. 4, 3.

[4]For writers maintaining this view, cf. *Concilium Tridentinum. Diariorum Actorum Epistularum Tractatuum nova collectio.* Ed. Societas Goerresiana, Vol. XII (Freiburg im Breisgau: Herder, 1929), p. 134, n. 5 (henceforth cited as *CT,* Vol. XII).

[5]Cf. *ibid.,* p. 135, n. 1.

[6]Cf. I Cor. 4, 1; Tit. 1, 7-9.

[7]Cf. Luke 12, 42.

[8]Cf. *Politics,* Book II, ch. 8, 23 (1296a), or Book IV, 4 (1292a).

[9]Matt. 10, 8.

[10]For legislation in this matter cf. *CT,* Vol. XII, p. 136, n. 1.

[11]The act of conferring a benefice or ecclesiastical office on a designated person.

[12]By Pope Clement VII in 1530; cf. *CT,* Vol. XII, p. 137, n. 2.

[13]Promises or reserving of benefices for new occupants before the death of the old holder.

[14]Conveyance of benefices by the pope. Cf. for example Jedin, *History of the Council of Trent,* Vol. I, p. 415, n. 4.

[15]Cf. *Corpus Iuris Canonici,* Vol. II (Graz: Akademische Druck=und Verlagsanstalt, 1959), cols. 1244-1245.

[16]Appointment as administrators.

[17]Cardinal Contarini in particular was concerned with the pastoral role of the bishop. He had written already in 1517 a treatise on the office and function of bishops: *De officio episcopi*, printed in his *Opera* (Paris: S. Nivelle, 1571), pp. 401-431. See also Gigliola Fragnito, "Cultura umanistica e riforma religiosa. Il 'De Officio viri boni ac probi episcopi' di Gasparo Contarini," *Studi Veneziani*, Vol. XI (1969), pp. 1-115, as well as Pierre Broutin, *L'évêque dans la tradition pastorale du XVIe siècle* (Bruges: Desclée de Brouwer, 1953).

[18]Cf. Matt. 6, 24; Luke 16, 13.

[19]For legislation concerning the residence of bishops, cf. Hubert Jedin, *History of the Council of Trent*, Vol. II (London: T. Nelson & Sons, 1961), pp. 317-318. Cardinal Cajetan in his commentary on St. Thomas Aquinas of the early sixteenth century maintained that the obligation of bishops to reside in their dioceses was based on divine law: cf. Hubert Jedin, "Der Kampf um die bischöfliche Residenzpflicht 1562-63," *Kirche des Glaubens, Kirche der Geschichte*, Vol. II (Freiburg im Breisgau: Herder, 1966), p. 402.

[20]The Council of Constance and the Fifth Lateran Council already tried to curb these practices: cf. *CT*, Vol. XII, p. 139, n. 2.

[21]Unreformed branches of mendicant orders.

[22]For existing legislation on this matter cf. *CT*, Vol. XII, p. 140, n. 1.

[23]Eccesiastics exercising the jurisdiction which is permanently and irremovably a part of their office. Cf. *The Oxford Dictionary of the Christian Church* (London: Oxford University Press, 1958), p. 990.

[24]This recommendation antedated by twenty-two years the *Index of Forbidden Books* of Pope Paul IV (1559), one of the authors of the *Consilium*.

[25]The *Colloquies* of Eramus were first printed in Basel in 1518. For a discussion of their publishing history, see *The Colloquies of Erasmus*, trans. by Craig R. Thompson (Chicago: University of Chicago Press, 1965), pp. xxi-xxxiii.

[26]A considerable body of papal orders against this abuse in individual cases already existed: cf. *CT*, Vol. XII, p. 141, n. 3. However, they set no precedent for effective general policy.

[27]The collectors mentioned here were sellers of indulgences, frequently members of charitable orders like that
of St. Anthony. While Luther had attacked indulgences as
such, the reform commission here turns only against financial abuses of the traffic in indulgences. For a brief
and succinct discussion of indulgence sellers with specific
reference to monks of St. Anthony, see Pierre Imbart de la
Tour, *Les origines de la Réforme*, Vol. II (Melun: Librairie
d'Argences, 1944), pp. 266-271. See also Nicolaus Paulus,
Geschichte des Ablasses im Mittelalter, Vol. II (Paderborn:
F. Schöningh, 1923), pp. 265-291.

[28]*Ibid.*, pp. 514-515 for a mention of this kind of
indulgences.

[29]Cf. the introduction to No. 1.

[30]See the introduction to No. 5.

[31]Born in 1477, Sadoleto became secretary to Pope Leo
X in 1513 and bishop of Carpentras in southern France in
1517. He continued his curial career under Pope Clement
VII. In 1536 he became a cardinal and an important proponent of church reform. He died in Rome in 1547. See
Richard M. Douglas, *Jacopo Sadoleto, 1477-1547: Humanist
and Reformer* (Cambridge, Mass.: Harvard University Press,
1959).

[32]Pole was a cousin of King Henry VIII of England. He
was born in 1500, studied in Oxford and Padua, and eventually broke his ties with Henry, remaining loyal to the
Roman church. He settled in Italy, became a cardinal in
1536 and governor of the *Patrimonium Petri*, a part of the
papal state, from 1541 to 1550. He returned to England as
papal legate in 1554 upon the accession of Queen Mary,
became archbishop of Canterbury in 1556, and died in 1558.
See W. Schenk, *Reginald Pole, Cardinal of England* (London:
Longmans, 1950). Dermot Fenlon, *Heresy and Obedience in
Tridentine Italy: Cardinal Pole and the Counter Reformation*
(Cambridge: Cambridge University Press, 1972). J. P.
Marmion, "Cardinal Pole in Recent Studies," *Recusant
History*, Vol. 13 (1975-76), pp. 56-61. Paolo Simoncelli,
Il caso Reginald Pole. Eresia e santità nelle polemiche
religiose del Cinquecento (Rome: Edizioni di Storia e
Letteratura, 1977).

[33]Fregoso was born in 1480 into a noble family of Genoa.
A scholar renowned for his knowledge of Greek and Hebrew,
he became archbishop of Salerno, bishop of Gubbio in 1533,
and cardinal in 1539. He died in 1541. No full bio-
graphy exists. For a brief sketch of his life see Luigi
Grillo, *Elogi di Liguri illustri*, 2d ed., Vol. I (Genoa:
Fratelli Ponthenier, 1846), pp. 390-398. M. Abbondanza,
"Federico Fregoso nella storia della diocesi di Salerno

e la visita pastorale del 1510-11," *Quaderni contemporanei*
[Salerno], Vol. 4 (1971), pp. 7-19.

[34]Aleandro or Aleander (1480-1542) in his younger
years was a friend of Erasmus. He became rector of the
University of Paris in 1513 and papal legate to Charles
V in 1521 in connection with the beginning of Luther's
career. He was made archbishop of Brindisi in 1524 and
cardinal in 1538. See *Dizionario biografico degli Italiani*,
Vol. II (Rome: Istituto della Enciclopedia Italiana,
1960), pp. 128-135 with bibliography.

[35]Giberti, born in Palermo in 1495, owed his curial
career to his friendship with Pope Clement VII, who
appointed him papal datary in 1523 and sent him on several
diplomatic missions. In 1524 he became bishop of Verona
where he took up residence in 1528. He was known as a
zealous reformer; his *Constitutiones* for Verona became a
model of rules governing diocesan administration and
pastoral activity. He died in Verona in 1543. See No.
5, n. 27 for bibliography.

[36]Cortese was born in Modena in 1483 and died in Rome
in 1548. He became a Benedictine monk and abbot of several
monasteries, including Lerins and San Giorgio Maggiore in
Venice. He was made cardinal in June, 1542, and became
bishop of Urbino in November of the same year. A modern
biography of Cortese is lacking. For bibliography, see
Marvin W. Anderson, "Gregorio Cortese and Roman Catholic
Reform," *Sixteenth Century Essays and Studies*, Vol. I
(St. Louis, Mo.: Forum Press, 1970), pp. 75-106.

[37]Badia, born in Modena in 1483, was a Dominican friar.
A teacher of theology, he was appointed papal theologian in
1529, with the title of "master of the sacred palace," and
eventually a member of the Roman Inquisition and censor
of books. A close friend and confessor of Contarini,
he became cardinal in 1542, and died in 1547. See
Dizionario biografico degli Italiani, Vol. V, pp. 74-76,
with bibliography.

NOTES

Chapter 7

[1]Pier Paolo Vergerio, as quoted in *The Benefit of Christ's Death*, edited by Churchill Babington (London, 1855), p. xli, mentions the probably exaggerated figure of forty thousand.

[2]Constantino Corvisieri, "Compendio dei processi del Santo Uffizio di Roma (da Paolo III a Paolo IV)," *Archivio della Società Romana di Storia Patria*, III (1880), p. 450.

[3]*Ibid.*, p. 274.

[4]*Ibid.*, p. 469.

[5]Benedetto da Mantova, *Il "Beneficio di Cristo" con le versioni del secolo XVI, documenti e testimonianze*, a cura di S. Caponetto [*Corpus Reformatorum Italicorum*, Vol. II] (Florence: Sansoni, and Chicago: The Newberry Library, 1972).

[6]Carlo Ginzburg - Adriano Prosperi, "Le due redazioni del 'Beneficio di Cristo'." *Eresia e Riforma nell'Italia del Cinquecento*, Miscellanea I [Biblioteca del Corpus Reformatorum Italicorum] (De Kalb, Ill.: Northern Illinois University Press and Chicago: The Newberry Library, 1974), pp. 135-204.

[7]For example, Dr. Prelowski in her edition makes numerous references to a limited number of works by the three northern reformers and Valdés. She cites the latter's *Alfabeto Cristiano* and *110 Divine Considerations* eighty-two times and refers the reader twenty times to Calvin's *Institutes*, eight times to Melanchthon's *Loci communes*, and thirty-six times to Luther's best-known works.

[8]Tommaso Bozza, *Il Beneficio di Cristo e la Istituzione della Religione Cristiana di Calvino*, (Rome, 1961). It was followed by *Introduzione al "Beneficio di Cristo"* (Rome, 1963), *Marco Antonio Flaminio e il "Beneficio di Cristo"* (Rome, 1966), *Calvino in Italia* (Rome, 1966), and *La Riforma cattolica. Il Beneficio di Cristo* (Rome: Libreria Tombolini 1972), all published by Arti Grafiche Italiane, except the last.

[9]See his classical article of 1929, translated as: "The Origins of the French Reformation: A badly-put question?", *A New Kind of History: from the writings of Febvre*, edited by Peter Burke (New York, Evanston, San Francisco: Harper and Row, 1973), pp. 44-107.

[10]Gen. I, 26-27.

[11]A theological term: incapable of suffering.

[12]Capable of suffering.

[13]Ps. CXV, 11; cf. Rom. III, 4.

[14]Ps. XIII, 3.

[15]Eph. II, 3.

[16]Cf. Gen. XVII, 4-9; Luke I, 55; Gal. III, 16.

[17]Deut. VI, 5; cf. Matt. XXII, 37; Mark XII, 30; Luke X, 27.

[18]Lev. XIX, 18; Matt. XXII, 39; Mark XII, 31; Luke X, 27.

[19]This may be a reference to the parable of the Good Samaritan, that follows the description of the Law in Luke's Gospel: cf. Luke X, 20-36.

[20]Cf. Rom. III, 20.

[21]Rom. VII, 7.

[22]Cf. Rom. VII, 5, 8.

[23]Cf. Rom. VII, 8-9.

[24]Gal. III, 10; cf. Deut. XXVII, 26.

[25]Cf. Rom. VII, 13; 2 Cor. III, 7.

[26]Rom. IV, 15.

[27]Rom. VIII, 7.

[28]Cf. Rom. X, 4.

[29]Cf. Exodus XX, 29: Deut. V, 25-27; XVIII, 16. This citation is a very free paraphrase of the Hebrews' statement, differing from all the scriptural versions of it.

[30]Cf. Deut. V, 28; XVIII, 17.

[31]Deut. XVIII, 18-19: cf. Acts III, 22-23.

[32]Cf. Col. III, 10.

[33]Acts IV, 12.

[34]Matt. XI, 28.

[35]John VII, 37.

[36]The author later discusses the imitation of Christ's life in more detail; see below, chapter V.

[37]John I, 29.

[38]Cf. Gal. III, 13.

[39]1 Cor. XV, 22.

[40]Cf. Ps. L, 5.

[41]Cf. 1 Cor. XV, 54-57: Hosea, XIII, 14.

[42]Rom. V, 12-21.

[43]Eph. II, 3.

[44]Cf. Rom. IX, 8: Gal. IV, 26.

[45]The author may have places such as these in mind: Augustine, *Enchiridion ad Laurentium*, cap. XXX (*Patrologia Latina*, vol. 40, col. 247); *De Fide et Operibus*, cap. XIV, 21. (PL 40,col. 211); *De Spiritu et Littera*, cap. X, 16. (PL 44, col. 210).

[46]Cf. 2 Cor. V, 20-21.

[47]Cf. Isaiah LIII, 1-7. The author omits part of verse 3.

[48]Gal. V, 4-5.

[49]The author's criticism of his opponents at this point is extremely sharp; he charges them with setting up humanly devised practices, such as indulgences, devotions, and pilgrimages, as the criteria of justification, in opposition both to God's will and to his Law.

[50]Cf. Heb. VII, 27; IX, 12, 28; X, 12, 14 and I John 1, 7; II, 2. The author obviously accepts Paul as the author of the epistle to the Hebrews.

[51]Phil. III, 6-10.

[52]Cf. 1 Cor. I, 30-31; the last phrase is the author's addition to the Scripture. Cf. 2 Cor. X, 17; Jer. IX, 23-24.

[53]Cf. Rom. VII, 1; Rom. VIII, 2.

[54]Cf. 1 Cor. II, 12-13; Rom. X, 4.

[55]A legal term; the simple contract written and signed by the debtor.

[56]Cf. Col. II, 14.

[57]Cf. 1 Cor. XV, 54-57: Hosea XIII, 14.

[58]Gen. III, 15.

[59]Gen. XXII, 18.

[60]Cf. Eph. V, 31.

[61]Cf. Eph. I, 20-21; Matt. XXVIII, 28.

[62]Cf. Eph. V, 25-27.

[63]John III, 16-18.

[64]Cf. Acts XV, 9.

[65]Cf. John III, 5; 1 Cor. III, 16.

[66]Cf. Rom. V, 15-17; 2 Cor. IX, 15; Eph. II, 8.

[67]Cf. Rom. VIII, 30.

[68]John VI, 39.

[69]John III, 14-15.

[70]John XI, 25-26.

[71]John XII, 46.

[72]Cf. 1 John IV, 8-10.

[73]Heb. II, 14-15.

[74]Cf. 1 Tim. III, 9; Eph. III, 4-5.

[75]Cf. Heb. IV, 16.

[76]Heb. X, 35.

[77]Heb. XI, 6.

[78]This is a reference to the argument in Hebrews, ch. II, where it is claimed that Old Testament figures possessed faith.

[79]Rom. IV, 3; Gen. XV, 6.

[80]Rom. III, 28.

[81]Rom. XI, 5-6.

[82]Gal. III, 11-12; cf. Habk. II, 4; Lev. XVIII, 5.

[83]Gal. II, 16.

[84]Gal. II, 21.

[85]Rom. X, 9-10.

[86]Cf. Augustine, *De Fide et Operibus*, cap. XVI, 27 (PL 40, col. 215). *De Spiritu et Littera*, cap. VII, 11 (PL 44, col. 206). *De diversis Quaestionibus octoginta tribus.* Quaest. LXXVI (PL 40, cols. 87-89). Epistolae Classis III, *Epistola ad Paulinum* (Bonifacium), CLXXXVI, 8ff. (PL 33, cols. 218-220). *Enarrationes in Psalmos*, Psalmus XXXI, Enar. II ff. (PL 36, col. 258, etc.).

[87]The citation given above for *De diversis Quaestionibus octoginta tribus* is concerned with this point.

[88]Luke VII, 47.

[89]Luke VII, 50.

[90]Isaiah LXIV, 6.

[91]Cf. Origen, *Commentarium in Epistolam ad Romanos*, Lib. III, 9 (Patrologia Graeca 14, cols. 952-954). The author mistakenly says the citation is from Book IV of this work.

[92]1 Cor. I, 30-31; cf. Jer. IX, 23-24.

[93]Basil, *Homilia de Humilitate*, XX, 3 (Patrologia Graeca 31, col. 530).

[94]Hilary, *Commentarius in Evangelium Matthei*, cap. VIII, 6 (PL 9, col. 961).

[95]Rom. IV, 5-6; cf. Psalm XXXI, 1-2.

[96]Cf. Luke X, 24; Matt. XIII, 7; cf. *Commentaria in Epistolas B. Pauli* (dubiously ascribed to Ambrose). *Ad Romanos*, cap. IV, ver. 5-6 (PL 17, cols. 86-87).

[97]Cf. Ambrose, *Commentaria in Epistolas B. Pauli; Ad Corinthianos primo*, cap. I, 4 (PL 17, cols. 194-195).

[98]Cf. Ambrose, Epistolae Classis II. *Epistola ad Irenaeum*, LXXIII, 11 (PL 16, col. 1038).

[99]Cf. Bernard, *Sermones in Cantica Canticorum*, Sermo LXVII (PL 183 [2], cols. 1107-1108). The author mistakenly cites the seventy-seventh sermon, but that is on a different topic.

[100]Cf. Gen. XXVII.

[101]Cf. Ambrose, *De Jacob et Vita Beata*, Lib. II, cap. II, 9 (PL 4, col. 648).

[102]Cf. Matt. XXII, 37, 39; Mark XII, 30-31; Luke X, 27.

[103]Psalm CXLII, 2.

[104]Prov. XX, 9.

[105]Job XV, 14-16.

[106]1 John I, 8.

[107]Matt. VI, 12; cf. Luke XI, 4.

[108]Luke XVII, 10.

[109]This may refer to the offering of masses for the dead and the granting of indulgences for the souls in purgatory.

[110]Cf. Acts XV, 9. The author mistakenly cites St. Paul instead of St. Peter.

[111]Cf. Matt. XXV, 34

[112]Cf. Eph. III, 17.

[113]Cf. Matt. XXVIII, 18.

[114]Cf. Matt. XXV, 3.

[115]Cf. Rom. VI, 6.

[116]Among other places, cf. Rom. I, 7; XV, 25; Eph. I, 1; 1 Cor. XIV, 33; Col. I, 2.

[117]Mark IX, 23.

[118]James II, 19.

[119]Cf. Rev. III, 17-18. The author has added interpretative comments to the text.

[120]James II, 18.

[121]Cf. among other places, Augustine, Epistolae, Classis III, *Epistola ad Sixtum*, cap. V, 19 (PL 33, col. 880); *Enarrationes in Psalmos*, In Psalmum CII, Enar. 7 (PL 37, cols. 1321-1322).

[122]John XVII, 20-22.

[123] Cf. Gal. III, 26-27.

[124] Cf. Rom. IV, 25.

[125] Heb. IX, 13-14.

[126] Cf. Matt. XII, 33, and Augustine, *De verbis Evangelii Matthei*, cap. XII, 33. Sermo LXII, 1 (PL 38, col. 467). Cf. also Matt. VII, 16-20.

[127] Cf. Rom. VIII, 29.

[128] Cf. Gal. VI, 14.

[129] Luke I, 74-75.

[130] Cf. Titus II, 11-13.

[131] Cf. Rom. VIII, 9.

[132] Cf. Gal. III, 26-27.

[133] Cf. Rom. VIII, 32.

[134] Cf. 1 Tim. III, 9.

[135] Ezechiel XXXVI, 26.

[136] 1 Peter II, 21.

[137] Cf. Eph. IV, 22-24.

[138] Rom. XIII, 12-14.

[139] Cf. Phil. II, 6, 8.

[140] Cf. Matt. XII, 19; Isaiah XLII, 2.

[141] Cf. 2 Tim. II, 23.

[142] Cf. 2 Tim. III, 12. Don Benedetto specifies the persecutors of the scriptural text as false Christians, indicating his consciousness of the split within Christianity itself.

[143] Cf. Luke XXIV, 34.

[144] Cf. Rom. XII, 5.

[145] Gal. V, 6.

[146] Luke IX, 23.

[147] Cf. 1 Peter I, 7.

[148]Cf. 2 Cor. XII, 9-10.

[149]2 Cor. IV, 7-10.

[150]Gal. VI, 14.

[151]Rom. V, 3-5; cf. James I, 4-5.

[152]Cf. 2 Cor. 1, 4; Psalm IX, 9-10.

[153]Cf. Rom. VIII, 17.

[154]Cor. I, 5.

[155]2 Tim. II, 12.

[156]Mark IX, 24.

[157]Luke XVII, 5.

[158]Cf. I Thess. V, 17; Luke XVIII, 1.

[159]Cf. I Peter III, 20-21.

[160]Mark XVI, 16.

[161]Cf. Gal. III, 27.

[162]Ps. XXXI, 1-2. Cf. Rom. IV, 6-8.

[163]Cf. Rom. X, 9-10.

[164]Matt. VI, 12; cf. Luke IX, 4.

[165]Luke XXII, 19; cf. Matt. XXVI, 26; Mark XIV, 22.

[166]Matt. XXVI, 28; cf. Luke XXII, 20; Mark XIV, 24.

[167]Gal. III, 15.

[168]Heb. IX, 15-17.

[169]Cf. John VI, 54.

[170]I Cor. XI, 27.

[171]I Cor. XI, 29.

[172]Rom. VIII, 33-34.

[173]Cf. Ps. CII, 1-13.

[174]Cf. Augustine, *In Joannis Evangelium* (PL 35, col. 1613).

[175]Augustine, *Sermones de Tempore*, cl. II, Sermo
CCLXXII (PL 38, col. 1246

[176]I Cor. X, 16-17.

[177]Cf. Rom. XII, 5.

[178]Luke X, 20.

[179]Cf. Rom. VIII, 29.

[180]Rom. VIII, 31.

[181]Rom. VIII, 35-37; Psalm XLIII, 22.

[182]Cf. I John III, 4-6.

[183]Cf. Luke X, 20.

[184]Heb. III, 6.

[185]Heb. X, 35.

[186]I John II, 1-2.

[187]Augustine, *De ecclesiasticis dogmatibus*, cap. LXXX
(PL 42, col. 1222).

[188]Prov. III, 12.

[189]Gal. III, 26; I Cor. III, 16.

[190]Eph. I, 13-14.

[191]Gal. III, 26.

[192]Gal. IV, 6.

[193]Rom. VIII, 14-17.

[194]Rom. VIII, 30-31.

[195]Cf. I Cor. II, 12.

[196]Cf. Rom. VIII, 9.

[197]Cf. I Cor. XII, 3.

[198]2 Cor. XIII, 5.

[199]John XIV, 17.

[200]Cf. Gal. V, 1-5.

[201]Eccles. IX, 1.

[202]I Cor. IV, 4.

[203]Cf. Eccles. III, 19.

[204]Cf. Psalm XVIII, 13.

[205]Cf. Rom. III, 28; V, 1.

[206]Phil. III, 9.

[207]2 Tim. IV, 8.

[208]Cf. Rom. VIII, 38-39.

[209]Cf. Phil. I, 23.

[210]Rom. VIII, 15.

[211]2 Tim. I, 7.

[212]Luke I, 70, 74-75.

[213]Rom. XIV, 17.

[214]Phil. IV, 4.

[215]Cf. I Peter I, 6, 8.

[216]Cf. Eph. IV, 30.

[217]Cf. Hilary, *Commentarium in Evangelium Matthei*,
cap. V, 6 (PL 9, cols. 944-945).

[218]Cf. James I, 6-8.

[219]Augustine, *Manuale*, cap. XXIII (PL 40, col. 961).

[220]*Ibid.*, cap. XIII (PL 40, col. 957).

[221]Bernard, *Sermones de sanctis, In Festo Annuntiationis
Beatae Mariae Virginis.* Sermo I, 1, 3 (PL 183, cols. 383-
384).

Chapter 8

[1]Agostino Mainardi; see introduction.

[2]There is a divergence in the extant manuscripts concerning this term: one reads "San Jacopo," the other "San Corpo." For a critical discussion of manuscripts of this tract, see Renato, *Opere*, pp. 291-297.

[3]Renato here stresses that there is no direct biblical statement which enjoins infant baptism.

[4]Cf., for example, Matt. 28, 19; Mark 16, 16; Acts 2, 38.

[5]Cf., for example, John 3, 5-6; Col. 2, 12-15; Gal. 6, 27; Tit. 3, 4-7.

[6]Cf., for example, Acts 2, 42; I Cor. 10, 16-18, and 11, 26.

[7]Acts 2, 41.

[8]Col. 1, 23.

[9]Acts 8, 36-39.

[10]Cf. Rom. 10, 11.

[11]Mark 16, 16.

[12]Matt. 19, 17.

[13]Cf. Gen. 17, 2.

[14]Cf. Mark 16, 16; John 3, 5.

[15]I Cor. 11, 26.

[16]Luke 22, 19; I Cor. 11, 24-25.

[17]2 Cor. 2, 11.

[18]Jer. 9, 5.

[19]James 1, 7.

[20]Acts 8, 38.

[21]Acts 15, 5.

[22]Rom. 4, 17.

[23]Matt. 26, 28.

[24]Jer. 31, 31-33.

[25]Hebr. 8-9.

[26]Hebr. 10, 5-7; cf. Ps. 40, 7-9.

[27]Exod. 12, 26-27.

[28]*Ibid.*, 12, 14.

[29]Eph. 2, 11.

[30]Gal. 3, 27-28.

[31]Rom. 10, 12; I Cor. 12, 13.

[32]Col. 2, 11.

[33]Rom. 10, 12.

SELECT BIBLIOGRAPHY

1. Bibliographical aids

Church, Frederic C. "The Literature of the Italian Reformation," *Journal of Modern History*, 3 (1931), pp. 457-
473.

Archive for Reformation History. Annual *Literature Review*,
beginning with 1972: section on Italy.

Rivista di Storia della Chiesa in Italia: each issue has
a bibliography in the back, arranged chronologically.

Archivum Historiae Pontificiae: rich bibliographies in
each annual volume, arranged according to papal reigns.

Revue d'Histoire Ecclésiastique: each issue has extensive
bibliographies arranged topically and chronologically.

*Bibliographie de la Réforme 1450-1648. Ouvrages parus de
1940 à 1955.* Volume 3: Italie - Espagne - Portugal
(Leiden: E. J. Brill, 1961).

Camaini, Pier Giorgio. "Interpretazioni della Riforma
cattolica e della Controriforma." *Grande Antologia
Filosofica*, ed. Michele Federico Sciacca, Volume VI
(Milan: Marzorati, 1964), pp. 329-490: rich bibliography.

_____. "Cinquecento religioso italiano e Concilio di
Trento," *Critica Storica*, 3 (1964), pp. 432-465.

Cervelli, Innocenzo. "Storiografia e problemi intorno alla
vita religiosa e spirituale a Venezia nella prima metà
del '500," *Studi Veneziani*, 8 (1966), pp. 447-476.

Chiminelli, Piero. *Bibliografia della storia della riforma
religiosa in Italia* (Rome: Casa Editrice Bilychnis,
1921; reprint, 1978): contains some errors.

Rosa, Mario. "Per la storia della vita religiosa e della
chiesa in Italia tra il '500 e '600. Studi recenti e
questioni di metodo," *Quaderni storici*, 15 (1970), pp.
673-758. Reprinted with slight changes in the author's
*Religione e società nel Mezzogiorno tra Cinque e Seicen-
to* (Bari: De Donato, 1976), pp. 75-155. Excellent discussion of recent research with rich bibliography in all
languages.

Simoncelli, Paolo. "Nuove ipotesi e studi sul 'Beneficio
    di Cristo'," *Critica Storica*, 12 (1975), pp. 321-388.

Gleason, Elisabeth G. "On the Nature of Sixteenth-Century
    Italian Evangelism: Scholarship, 1953-1978," *The
    Sixteenth Century Journal*, 9 (1978), pp. 3-25.

2. General Works

Cantimori, Delio. "Italy and the Papacy," *The New Cambridge
    Modern History*, Vol. 2: *The Reformation, 1520-1559*,
    ed. G. R. Elton (Cambridge: University Press, 1958),
    pp. 251-274.

Brucker, Gene. *Renaissance Florence* (New York: John Wiley
    and Sons, 1969): chapter five.

Cochrane, Eric, ed. *The Late Italian Renaissance, 1525-1630*
    (New York, Evanston, London: Harper and Row, 1970),
    Part III: "Reformation and Counter Reformation."

Hay, Denys. *The Church in Italy in the Fifteenth Century*
    (Cambridge: University Press, 1977). Although dealing
    with an earlier period, useful material for the
    sixteenth century can be found in chapters 4, 5, and 6.

Grendler, Paul. *Critics of the Italian World, 1530-1560*
    (Madison, Milwaukee and London: The University of
    Wisconsin Press, 1969): chapter six.

Ortolani, Oddone. "The Hopes of the Italian Reformers in
    Roman Action," *The Proceedings of the Unitarian Histori-
    cal Society*, Vol. XIV, Parts I and II (1962-1963):
    *Italian Reformation Studies in Honor of Laelius
    Socinus (1562-1962)*, ed. John Tedeschi, pp. 11-20.

Partner, Peter. *Renaissance Rome, 1500-1559* (Berkeley and
    Los Angeles: University of California Press, 1976):
    chapters one and four.

Prodi, Paolo. "The Structure and Organization of the
    Church in Renaissance Venice: Suggestions for Research,"
    Renaissance Venice, ed. J. R. Hale (London: Faber and
    Faber, 1973), pp. 409-430.

Miccoli, Giovanni. "La storia religiosa," *Storia d'Italia*,
    Vol. 2 (Torino: Giulio Einaudi editore, 1974), pp. 431-
    1079: especially pp. 975-1079.

Penco, Gregorio. *Storia della Chiesa in Italia*, Vol. I
    (Milan: Jaca Book, 1978).

3. Works on the Reformation in Italy

Brown, G. K. *Italy and the Reformation to 1550* (Oxford:
    Blackwell, 1933).

Church, Frederic C., *The Italian Reformers, 1534-1564*
    (New York: Columbia University Press, 1932; reprint,
    New York: Octagon Books, 1974).

Bainton, Roland. *Women of the Reformation in Germany and
    Italy* (Minneapolis: Augsburg Publishing House, 1971).

McLelland, Joseph C., ed., *Peter Martyr Vermigli and
    Italian Reform* (Waterloo, Ontario: Wilfrid Laurier
    University Press, 1980).

McNair, Philip. *Peter Martyr in Italy. An Anatomy of
    Apostasy* (Oxford: Clarendon Press, 1967).

Nieto, José C. *Juan de Valdés and the Origins of the
    Spanish and Italian Reformation* (Geneva: Droz, 1970).

Schutte, Anne J. *Pier Paolo Vergerio: the Making of an
    Italian Reformer* (Geneva: Droz, 1977).

Rotondò, Antonio. *Calvin and the Italian Anti-Trinitarians*.
    Translated by John and Anne Tedeschi (St. Louis, Mo.:
    Foundation for Reformation Research, 1968).

Williams, George H. *The Radical Reformation* (Philadelphia:
    The Westminster Press, 1962), passim.

Benrath, Karl. *Die Reformation in Venedig* (Halle: Verein
    für Reformationsgeschichte, 1887): still valuable

Berengo, Marino. *Nobili e mercanti nella Lucca del
    Cinquecento* (Turin: Einaudi, 1965): see chapter "La
    vita religiosa," pp. 357-454.

Bozza, Tommaso. *Nuovi studi sulla riforma in Italia. I.
    Il Beneficio di Cristo* (Rome: Edizioni di Storia e
    Letteratura, 1976).

Buisson, Ferdinand. *Sébastien Castellion. Sa vie et son
    oeuvre (1515-1563)* (The Hague: Nieuwkoop, 1964 reprint).

Buschbell, Gottfried. *Reformation und Inquisition in
    Italien um die Mitte des XVI. Jahrhunderts* (Paderborn:
    F. Schöningh, 1910).

Cantimori, Delio. *Eretici Italiani del Cinquecento*
    (Florence: Sansoni, 1939). Classic work which in-
    fluenced all subsequent scholarship.

_____. *Prospettive di storia ereticale italiana del
    Cinquecento* (Bari: Laterza, 1960).

_____. "La Riforma in Italia," *Problemi storici e orientamenti storiografici*, ed. E. Rota (Como: Cavalleri, 1942), pp. 557-584.

_____. "Le idee religiose del Cinquecento: la storiografia," in *Storia della letteratura italiana*, a cura di E. Cecchi and N. Sapegno, Vol. V: *Il Seicento* (Milan: Garzanti, 1967), pp. 7-87.

_____. *Umanesimo e religione nel Rinascimento* (Turin: Einaudi, 1975): collected essays.

Caponetto, Salvatore, *Aonio Paleario e la Riforma protestante in Toscana* (Turin: Claudiana Editrice, 1979).

Chabod, Federico. *Per la storia religiosa dello Stato di Milano durante il dominio di Carlo V*. Note e documenti. 2d ed. (Rome: Istituto Storico Italiano per l'Età Moderna e Contemporanea, 1962).

De Maio, Romeo. *Riforme e miti nella Chiesa del Cinquecento* (Naples: Guida, 1973): essays dealing with aspects of sixteenth century Italian religious history.

Ginzburg, Carlo. *Il Nicodemismo. Simulazione e dissimulazione religiosa nell'Europa del '500* (Turin: Einaudi, 1970).

_____. *I benandanti. Stregoneria e culti agrari tra Cinquecento e Seicento* (Turin: Einaudi, 1972).

_____. *Il formaggio e i vermi*. Il cosmo di un mugnaio del '500 (Turin: Einaudi, 1976). An English version in: James Obelkevich, ed., *Religion and the People, 800-1700* (Chapel Hill, N.C.: University of North Carolina Press, 1979). Now translated by J. and A. Tedeschi, *The Cheese and the Worms* (Baltimore, Md.: The Johns Hopkins University Press, 1980).

Kutter, M. *Celio Secondo Curione, sein Leben und sein Werk* (1503-1569) (Basel and Stuttgart: Schwabe, 1955).

Marchetti, Valerio. *Gruppi ereticali senesi del Cinquecento* (Florence: La Nouva Italia, 1975).

Ortolani, Oddone. *Per la Storia della vita religiosa italiana nel Cinquecento. Pietro Carnesecchi* (Florence: Le Monnier, 1963).

Paladino, Giuseppe, ed. *Opuscoli e lettere di riformatori italiani del Cinquecento*, 2 Vols. (Bari: Laterza, 1913).

Peyronel Rambaldi, Susanna, *Speranze e crisi nel Cinquecento Modenese* (Milan: Franco Angeli Editore, 1979).

Pommier, Édouard. "La société vénitienne et la Reforme
    Protestante au XVIe siècle," *Bollettino dell' Istituto
    di Storia e dello Stato Veneziano*, Vol. I (1959), pp.
    3-26.

Rotondò, Antonio. *Studi e ricerche di storia ereticale
    italiana del Cinquecento*, I (Turin: Edizioni
    Giappichelli, 1974).

_____. "La censura ecclesiastica e la cultura,"
    Storia d'Italia, Vol. V, 2 (I documenti) (Turin:
    Einaudi, 1973), pp. 1397-1492.

Sta. Terresa, Domingo de. *Juan de Valdés 1498?-1541. Su
    pensamiento religioso y las corrientes espirituales de
    su tiempo* (Rome: Gregorian University, 1957).

Stella, Aldo. *Dall'anabattismo al socinianesimo nel
    Cinquecento veneto. Ricerche storiche* (Padua: Liviana
    Editrice, 1967).

_____. *Anabattismo e antitrinitarismo in Italia nel
    XVI secolo* (Padua: Liviana Editrice, 1969).

Simoncelli, Paolo. *Evangelismo italiano del Cinquecento.
    Questione religiosa e nicodemismo politico* (Rome:
    Istituto Storico Italiano per l'Età Moderna e Contem-
    poranea, 1979).

4. Works on the Counter-Reformation which contribute
    especially to an understanding of sixteenth-century
    Italy:

Cochrane, Eric. "New Light on Post-Tridentine Italy: a
    Note on Recent Counter-Reformation Scholarship,"
    Catholic Historical Review, Vol. 56 (1970-71), pp.
    291-319.

Dickens, A. G. *The Counter Reformation* (New York: Harcourt,
    Brace and World, 1969): good brief discussion of
    movements for reform before the Council of Trent.

Delumeau, Jean. *Catholicism Between Luther and Voltaire:
    a New View of the Counter-Reformation* (Philadelphia:
    Westminster, 1977): provocative thesis.

Douglas, Richard. *Jacopo Sadoleto, 1477-1547: Humanist and
    Reformer* (Cambridge, Mass.: Harvard University Press,
    1959).

Fenlon, Dermot. *Heresy and Obedience in Tridentine Italy.
    Cardinal Pole and the Counter Reformation* (Cambridge:
    Cambridge University Press, 1972).

Jedin, Hubert. *History of the Council of Trent*, Vol. I,
    tr. by E. Graf (St. Louis: Herder, 1957): excellent
    discussion of reform efforts at the curia before 1545.